MARY BAR

David Edgar's first major pla[...]
story — the story of Mary Ba[...]
her emergence from it with [...]
of the anti-psychiatric schoo[...]

Reviewing the premiere produc[...]
Michael Billington wrote: 'The play begins in 1965. [...]
a rambling East End house taken over by a group of psycho-
therapists who want, as someone says, "to avoid the kind of mental
health that gets its kicks from putting things into people". Edgar
traces the help given to Mary Barnes, a 42-year-old girl who has
previously been diagnosed as schizophrenic. Gradually we see
Mary, in the context of an extended family, transformed from a
wilful, tantrum-filled, attention-grabbing elderly child into
someone freed from the tyranny of self and capable of exercising
protective care of others . . . What is refreshing is that it is a play
about mental illness with no shibboleths, no slogans, no facile
answers: simply a specific, well-documented account of one
treatment that worked.'   (*The Guardian*)

'It is a harrowing play, passionate and compassionate.'
                                           (John Peter, *Sunday Times*)

'David Edgar's approach is meticulous and his study always
absorbing.'   (*Keith Nurse, Daily Telegraph*)

'This is David Edgar's finest play to date . . . '
                               (Anthony Everitt, *Birmingham Post*)

*The photo on the front cover shows Patti Love as Mary Barnes in
the Birmingham Rep Studio production and is reproduced by
courtesy of Willoughby Gullachsen. The photo of David Edgar on
the back cover is by Nobby Clark.*

by the same author

WRECKERS (*Eyre Methuen*, 1977)

DESTINY (*Eyre Methuen*, 1978)

DICK DETERRED (*Monthly Review Press, New York*, 1974)

TWO KINDS OF ANGEL (in *The London Fringe Theatre, Burnham House*, 1975)

THE JAIL DIARY OF ALBIE SACHS (*Rex Collings*, 1978)

BALL BOYS (*Pluto Press*, 1978)

David Edgar

Mary Barnes

Based on "Mary Barnes: Two Accounts of a Journey through Madness" by Mary Barnes and Joseph Berke

EYRE METHUEN · LONDON

First published in 1979 by Eyre Methuen Ltd, 11 New Fetter Lane,
London EC4P 4EE
Copyright © 1979 by David Edgar
ISBN 0 413 40070 0

Set IBM 🅕 Tek-Art, Croydon, Surrey.
Printed in Great Britain by Cox & Wyman Ltd.,
London, Fakenham & Reading.

To my Mother and Father

Author's Note

Mary Barnes: Two Accounts of a Journey Through Madness is a true story, set in the recent past, about a group of people who believed fiercely in a particular view of the nature of madness, and who attempted to live that belief in a peculiarly intense and passionate way. This has led to problems in adapting the book for the stage. The first was that I needed to fictionalize the characters in the book in order to give myself the freedom to represent their community dramatically. Mary Barnes and Joseph Berke quoted, liberally and in retrospect, third parties. I have gone further, and invented many statements and actions by people involved in Mary's journey. For this reason, Mary Barnes herself is the only named character in the play. Other people often say and do things that were really said and done; what the characters *are*, however, is my own invention.

Second, the exigencies of time and clarity forced me to telescope and even alter many of the events in the book, to combine functions and people, and to find ways of making publicly clear what was occurring in the privacy of people's minds and souls.

I should like to thank Mary Barnes and Joseph Berke for their tireless patience with my questions, and for their generosity in accepting my interpretation of their story. I must also acknowledge my gratitude to Peter Farago, who not only realized the play as its director, but who also contributed, above and beyond the call of duty, to its writing. And, finally, my thanks to Patti Love, who suggested the project in the first place, and whose performance in the name part was as near perfection as I had always, quite unreasonably, expected it to be.

David Edgar

MARY BARNES was first presented at the Birmingham Repertory
Theatre Studio on 31 August 1978, with the following cast:

LECTURER	Roger Allam
NURSE	Judith Harte
SIMON	David Gant
DOUGLAS	Tim Hardy
KEITH	Teddy Kempner
BRENDA	Ann Mitchell
MARY	Patti Love
HUGO	Donald Sumpter
ZIMMERMAN	Alan Aldred
EDDIE	Simon Callow
BETH	Katherine Kitovitz
LAURENCE	Timothy Spall
ANGIE	Judy Monahan
ANGIE'S MOTHER	Judith Harte
ANGIE'S BROTHER	Roger Allam

Directed by Peter Farago
Designed by Andrea Montag
Lighting by Mick Hughes

The set is divided into two areas, connected by stairs. Downstairs
is a general living and eating space, with exits to the kitchen, the
stairs and the street. Upstairs is a bedroom, with an iron bedstead
and washstand. At the beginning of the play, the set is almost
empty; by the end of the first act, it has developed the fittings
of occupation. The play takes place in a large old house in East
London and starts in 1965.

This is the text of the Birmingham Rep Studio production.

Act One

Scene One

White screens, as a frontcloth, conceal the main set. In front of the screens is a lectern, with microphone.
Beside the lectern is a chair. As the houselights fade, a NURSE brings on a middle-aged male mental PATIENT who sits in the chair. The NURSE stands at the side.

Stage lights fade up as a LECTURER comes to the lectern. He addresses the audience. He speaks from notes.

LECTURER. Good afternoon. Modern theories of the disorder or disorders labelled schizophrenia are based on a clinical model. Once, we considered schizophrenics either bad, malevolent, or mad, possessed by demons. Now, we all accept that they are medically ill, and therefore curable. Yes?

NURSE. Simple schizophrenia. Flatness of affect. He doesn't want to tell us what he feels.

LECTURER. Yes.

Slight pause.

This doesn't mean, of course, that schizophrenia's the same as mumps or flu, the sufferer from which is well aware that he's unwell. Most schizophrenics are, in fact, quite unaware that they're unwell. Indeed, the more unwell they are, the greater is their unawareness of that fact. Furthermore, it is the vehement refusal of the patient to admit he's ill at all that provides us with the clue to his condition. And?

NURSE. Catatonia. Stupor. He refuses to communicate.

LECTURER. Mm.

Slight pause.

Most people now accept that schizophrenia results from bio-chemical disfunction in the brain. One theory argues that excessive dopamine activity may be the casual factor. But, whatever system is malfunctioning, once we've found out, it's one small step to correct the error and make it work again. Go on.

NURSE. Hebephrenia. Depersonalization. He thinks he's a machine.

LECTURER. I see.

Slight pause.

This patient, in his forties. Mental hospital for many years. A clever child, artistic, manually dextrous, schizophrenic symptoms in his middle teens. Ambivalence, withdrawal, and inertia. Later, hyperkinesis and looseness of association. At the age of 20, asked his sister if she'd go to bed with him, the family informed the medical authorities, committed to a mental hospital. That's all?

NURSE. There's paranoia. There's delusions. Thinks that people plot against him. And —

The LECTURER waves the NURSE on.

He thinks he's being tortured, and he thinks he's being poisoned.

LECTURER. Treatment?

NURSE. With electric shocks and insulin.

LECTURER. Indeed.

Pause.

In fact, we don't know how they work.

Slight pause.

In fact, we don't know quite how aspirin works.

Slight pause. Firmly:

We know they stop the pain.

The LECTURER picks up his notes and goes out. The NURSE takes the PATIENT out. Blackout and the screens are struck.

Scene Two

Immediately, in the DARKNESS, the first few bars of the Beatles' "Dizzy Miss Lizziy", performed energetically but inaccurately. It peters out in a mass of wrong notes, lack of rhythm and feedback.
  LIGHTS. *The main set. The microphone is the only thing remaining from the previous scene. In the room, also, a side-drum, cymbal, and a screwdriver on the floor.*
  DOUGLAS, *who is 30, dressed in a three-piece suit, stands. He carries a good quality suitcase and briefcase. He puts them down, looks round. He taps the head of the microphone. It's dead. He can't work out what it's doing there. He notices a mirror, in the fourth wall. He looks at himself, his neatness, his suit.*
  From offstage, the same burst of Beatles, petering out.

DOUGLAS *looks off, towards the noise. Then looks at the mirror.*
Decision. He lays down his suitcase, opens it, takes out a floppy
old sweater, on which is pinned a CND badge, a pair of suede shoes
and a coathanger. He takes off his jacket, waistcoat and shoes. He
hangs the jacket, waistcoat and tie on the hanger and, there being
nowhere else, hangs it on the mikestand. The same burst of music.
DOUGLAS *looks towards it, then puts on the sweater and suedes. He*
looks at himself in the mirror. He ruffles his hair.

    Enter, right, KEITH, *a teenager in a collarless Beatle jacket. He's*
about to speak when DOUGLAS, *who hasn't noticed him, pulls a*
face in the mirror, and flops his body about, as if to affirm his
liberation from the suited attire.

    KEITH, *stopped in his tracks, waits a moment, uncertain. Then,*
feeling the need to advertise his presence, if only to save future
embarrassment, he coughs.

KEITH. Erm . . .

    DOUGLAS *turns.*

    Erm . . .

DOUGLAS (*not embarrassed by the interruption of his ritual*).
Yes?

KEITH. Erm . . . Our mike.

    DOUGLAS *doesn't understand.* KEITH *points at the mike and*
    the drums.

    Our mike, and our drums. Our group.

DOUGLAS. Oh, yes.

    DOUGLAS *takes the suit from the mike stand, with a slightly*
    theatrical gesture.

KEITH. Ta.

    KEITH *takes the mikestand, and, with some difficulty, picks*
    up the drum and cymbal as well, shakes his head at DOUGLAS's
    gesture of help, and goes out right. DOUGLAS, *left holding the*
    coathanger with nowhere to hang it, goes out. "Dizzy Miss
    Lizzy" *bursts out again. Goes on a little longer, but still peters*
    out. Enter BRENDA, *left. She's 33, with a slight Yorkshire*
    accent. She notices DOUGLAS's *luggage. Calls.*

BRENDA. Hugo? Duggie? Who is it?

    Re-enter DOUGLAS, *hangerless.*

DOUGLAS. Brenda. I'm the first?

BRENDA. Duggie. More or less. 'Cept for Zimmerman.

DOUGLAS. Zimmerman?

BRENDA. In the basement. Playing with his skooba box.

DOUGLAS. What in God's name is a skooba box?

BRENDA. Not easy to divine. Empirically, it's a large, black wooden box, with lights inside which flash on and off when you sit in it. Essentially, I gather it's more to do with meditation, mind expansion, and the hidden breathing one-ness of the cosmos. The discovery thereof. He calls it an environment.

DOUGLAS. Ah. Reich.

BRENDA. Third?

DOUGLAS. No. Wilhelm.

BRENDA. Doubtless. D'you want some —

DOUGLAS. Artists.

BRENDA. Eh?

DOUGLAS (*going to shut his case*). You try to escape, move to the East End, somewhere on the nether reaches of the District Line, beyond the writ of civilization, and what happens? Artists, they're there before you.

BRENDA. Yuh.

Pause. They smile at each other. Doorbell rings.

I'll go.

Exit BRENDA left. "Dizzy Miss Lizzy" once more. This time, however, only a bar before chaos. Almost immediately, enter KEITH, who, seeing DOUGLAS, treats him with some nervousness.

DOUGLAS. Problems?

KEITH. Eh?

DOUGLAS. The song. You sound like you got problems.

KEITH. Erm, yuh. Only, a. Fuse gone. Won't take a second to, um.

He is looking around. He spots the screwdriver on the floor, picks it up with some relief, as enters BRENDA.

BRENDA. Oh, Keith. There's a lady, lots of luggage. Would you be a love?

KEITH. Beg pardon? Be a what?

BRENDA. Give her a hand.

KEITH *looks towards the group, then shrugs.*

KEITH. Oh, yuh, sure. Why not.

KEITH *goes out left, pocketing the screwdriver.*

DOUGLAS. Ringo?

BRENDA *queries,* DOUGLAS *gestures off left.*

BRENDA. Oh, Keith. It's a Youth Club thing, they come in every week, apparently, to practise.

DOUGLAS. Need to.

BRENDA. Hasn't been established, now we're . . .

DOUGLAS. We ought to keep as many local links as —

BRENDA. Otherwise, what is the point of moving here.

DOUGLAS. Exactly.

Enter KEITH with a suitcase and portable typewriter. He puts them down.

KEITH. Well. Here we —

BRENDA. Upstairs? First on left?

KEITH (*picks up the luggage*). First on. The left.

He goes out to the stairs. Enter MARY. She's 42, dressed in a nursing sister's uniform, her hair neatly pinned up. She carries a small suitcase and a vanity case.

MARY. Duggie.

DOUGLAS. Hallo, love.

MARY. Where am I?

BRENDA. Show you.

Bell rings. DOUGLAS *exits left.* MARY *follows* BRENDA *towards the stairs. Then* KEITH *appears.*

BRENDA. Thanks, Keith.

MARY. Oh, yes. Thank you.

KEITH. Not at all.

MARY and BRENDA go upstairs. KEITH going out right, when DOUGLAS enters with HUGO. HUGO is in his late-30s. He too wears a suit.

HUGO. Good afternoon.

KEITH. Good . . . Hi.

Exit KEITH *quickly.* HUGO *looks at* DOUGLAS.

HUGO. Who?

DOUGLAS. The local Beatle-boys.

HUGO. I see.

DOUGLAS. When's Eddie coming?

HUGO. I don't know. Last heard of, doing something counter-cultural in San Francisco.

DOUGLAS. Doing it to whom?

HUGO. He didn't say.

Enter BRENDA *from the stairs.*

BRENDA. Hugo.

HUGO. Brenda. Everything all right?

BRENDA. Well, more or less. I've even got the central heating kind of working.

HUGO. Kind of?

BRENDA. Only kind of central heating.

Pause. The THREE *look at each other.*

Well.

HUGO. Well, here we are.

DOUGLAS. Lease signed.

BRENDA. Our occupancy —

DOUGLAS. Staked.

HUGO. Our place.

BRENDA. Our liberated zone.

A VOICE (*off*). Aha!

DOUGLAS. Eh?

Enter ZIMMERMAN. *He is in his 20s. He wears his hair long for 1965. He is dressed in an old sweater, corduroy trousers, sandles and elastoplasted spectacles. A row of fairy lights hangs round his neck. He carries a lead.*

ZIMMERMAN. Discovered. A cell of mad psychiatrists.

BRENDA. I beg your pardon?

ZIMMERMAN. What would you say, assemblage? As in school of porpoises or pride of lions. Cell's not right. Um — ego? P'raps an anal? No, I have it. Trauma. I have stumbled on a trauma of psychiatrists.

DOUGLAS. You what?

ZIMMERMAN. I need a screwdriver. My environment has just shortcircuited. You don't, on any of your persons . . . ?

DOUGLAS. Try the pop group.

ZIMMERMAN. Fine.

Exit ZIMMERMAN.

BRENDA. Zimmerman.

DOUGLAS. What a pretty name.

HUGO. He changed it, by deed poll, from Dylan Roberts. So he claims. He couldn't stand the strain.

DOUGLAS. The strain of what?

BRENDA. I'll put the kettle on.

Exit BRENDA *left.*

HUGO. We should meet and eat in here. I mean, every night. We must avoid hierarchies, chains of authority, unspoken rules. Or we should at least speak our unspoken rules.

Re-enter ZIMMERMAN *with the screwdriver.*

DOUGLAS. Successful?

ZIMMERMAN. Very odd.

HUGO. What way?

ZIMMERMAN. Well, I went in, and, I thought quite politely, asked if they had such a thing as a screwdriver. Dead silence. So I asked again, d'you have a screwdriver, cos I seem to have a short in my environment. Another silence, and then one of them just thrusts this at me, almost desperately, saying, take it, have it, please don't fag returning it, it's yours.

MARY *appears from the stairs.*

Well, I ask you. Barmy. Got to be.

He sits and unscrews the plug from the socket.

MARY. Hallo, Doctor.

HUGO. Oh, hallo. I didn't know you'd come.

MARY. Oh, I arrived a short time previously.

She sits.

HUGO. Are you still, working at the hospital?

MARY. I am. But I'm applying for a nearer job. To save on travelling.

HUGO. That's good.

Enter KEITH.

MARY. Yes? Can we help you?

KEITH. Erm . . .

Sees ZIMMERMAN.

Oh, uh . . .

Thinks of an alternative question. To MARY:

Wondered if us, the group, I mean, if we could come here, now you've, erm . . .

Vague gesture at ZIMMERMAN, *who looks up from his work and smiles pleasantly.*

You've moved your people in.

BRENDA *enters with mugs of tea, a bottle of milk and a bag of sugar on a tray, as:*

MARY. That's fine by me.

KEITH. Oh, ta —

MARY. But you must ask Dr Walker.

KEITH *looks round, trying to work out which is* DR WALKER.

KEITH (*to* HUGO). Erm —

DOUGLAS. Yes, it's fine. Come in whenever you want.

KEITH. Oh. Ta.

MARY. Brenda, jug.

BRENDA. I'm sorry?

MARY. You should use a jug, for milk, and sugar in a bowl, not just a scrappy paper bag.

BRENDA. I —

MARY. Now I want, please, to discuss my place here.

Pause. KEITH *stays, watching.*

HUGO (*sits*). Go on.

MARY. You see, I feel that all this must be sorted out. Regarding, in particular, finance. You see, I need to know how all of you, this place, is situated. I would say, for instance, I earn now about one thousand and four hundred pounds, you see. And I'd suggest that I receive, say twenty pounds a week, of which I'd pay some rent, five pounds, with fifteen net. But there is also my expense account.

HUGO. Yuh.

MARY. Well, often, you see, need to, in my room, my kind of office, need to entertain, professionals, buy wine, cigars, and also in the room that's next to mine, I'd like to keep, for guests, e.g. my father if he came to work about the house, in my capacity, if anyone was ill, a patient in the house, I'd have them to my room and give them, tablets or hot milk or penicillin, as the need arose, and sleep, they'd sleep there, in my room or in my bed, you see, and . . .

Pause.

Trust all that is satisfactory.

BRENDA. Sure. D'you want some tea?

MARY. No, Brenda, tea is wrong.

HUGO. All right. You needn't have it.

Pause.

MARY. Now I have a study to complete. Case study, to complete this evening. You'll forgive me.

MARY *stands and goes out to the stairs.*

KEITH. Eh. She's looney.

HUGO. Yes, that's right.

KEITH. But she —

HUGO. She doesn't —

KEITH. Doesn't?

HUGO. Know. She doesn't know —

KEITH. She doesn't know?

HUGO. She's —

KEITH. Looney. Doesn't know she's looney.

HUGO. Yes. Precisely.

KEITH. Ah. Oh. Right.

Exit KEITH.

DOUGLAS. Should she?

HUGO. Should she?

DOUGLAS. Know.

HUGO. Yes. Yes, she should.

> DOUGLAS *drains his tea, stands and exits to the stairs. Pause.*

HUGO. A Nato officer was on a naval exercise. Polaris. He refused to press the button. Said that no man should be so commanded. Diagnosed as schizophrenic, put in mental hospital.

BRENDA. Whereas the person, President, Prime Minister, controls the bomb, for real, and threatens to explode it, he is obviously sane.

ZIMMERMAN (*stands*). That's it. Loose wire. I think I'll chance it, plug it in.

> ZIMMERMAN *plugs his lead into a wall-plug. The fairy-lights come on and fade with the quick blackout.*

Scene Three

Upper area. MARY *sits at a table, typing. On the table, a picture of a nun.* DOUGLAS *stands, smoking.*

DOUGLAS. What you doing?

MARY. Oh, I'm working on a study. For the *Nursing Times*.

DOUGLAS. Oh, good.

MARY. I've got to get it in the post tonight.

DOUGLAS. Oh, fine.

> *He picks up the picture.*

Who's this?

MARY. It's St Theresa. Of Lisieux.

DOUGLAS. What did she do?

MARY. She was a nun. The nineteenth century. She died at 24. TB.

DOUGLAS. Why was she made a saint?

> *Pause.*

MARY. I had an interview, today, a nearer hospital. They said they might employ me.

DOUGLAS. Great.

MARY. This article. Must pop out to the post, tonight.

DOUGLAS. Pop out.

MARY. She was, just ordinary. Simple. Good. An ordinary, unknown girl, who happened to be good enough to be a saint. Now, if you'll forgive me . . .

DOUGLAS. Yuh.

Slight pause.

Pop out?

MARY *looks at him.*

Go out? Out, Mary?

Pause. MARY *very still.*

MARY. Duggie.

DOUGLAS. It's OK.

MARY. I've come —

DOUGLAS. Don't worry —

MARY. Come to have a breakdown.

Pause. Quickly, MARY *pulls out the sheet in the typewriter, puts in another sheet, types.*

Dear — Matron — Thank — you — for — the — interview — but — now — I'm — otherwise — engaged — Yours.

She takes out the paper, signs it.

Mary Barnes.

Pause. MARY *reaches to her hair, pulls out the pins. Her hair falls down.*

I'm cold.

The Beatle-boys finally get Dizzy Miss Lizzy together. DOUGLAS *looks towards the sound.* MARY *still.* BLACKOUT.

Scene Four

In the DARKNESS, *a male American* VOICE.

VOICE. Hey!

Slight pause. Something falls over.

Hey! Hey!

Noise of SOMEONE *moving about in an unfamiliar dark room.*

Hey, anybody home?

ZIMMERMAN (*in the DARKNESS*). I'm home. You're standing on my home.

> LIGHTS. *Main area.* BRENDA, *in her nightclothes, stands by the stairs exit, having just switched the* LIGHTS *on. The* VOICE, EDDIE, *is standing on the mattress on which, in his sleeping bag,* ZIMMERMAN *was sleeping.* EDDIE *is 25.* BETH, *another young American, stands nearby. Luggage about the place. It was a suitcase that fell over.*

EDDIE. Brenda.

BRENDA. Ah. It's you.

EDDIE (*to* ZIMMERMAN). Hey, I'm sorry.

ZIMMERMAN (*sits up, puts on his glasses*). Don't mention it.

BRENDA. How d'you get in?

EDDIE. The window.

> BRENDA *marching across the room.*

BRENDA. Right. We fix the window.

EDDIE. Brenda, this is Beth.

BRENDA. Hi Beth.

EDDIE (*following* BRENDA). We met on this plane. I brought her here. Beth tells me she's a career loco and she's —

BETH. Unhappy in my work.

EDDIE. Unhappy in her —

BRENDA (*turning to* EDDIE). It is half past —

> EDDIE, *suddenly, grandly, picking up a case and plonking it on the table.*

EDDIE. For we did hear it whispered, that the centre of the human consciousness, was not among the mantrad mountain-peaks of Hindu Kush, nor yet amid the San Franciscan Friaries of Northern California, nor, even yetter, as one Ginsberg, Allen, paraphrenically put it, Liverpool —

BRENDA. Look, why don't you —

EDDIE (*opening his case*). But in a crumbling fortress in East London, peopled by all classes and varities of freak and leper, most if not all described as psychotherapist, all if not most quite certifiably insane . . .

BRENDA. Look, it is very —

EDDIE. Where, we heard it whispered, secretly, whatever it is is now at. Thus we pursued it, hither, following the star, across the oceons.

BRENDA sits.

There being something of a shortage, in the excise-free, of frankinsense and myrhh, with gifts of liquid gold.

EDDIE takes a bottle from the case. BETH is checking her A to Z against a piece of paper.

Tequila. Mexican. Distilled from cactus. Perforates the mind.

He puts the bottle on a chair.

The spikes go straight through the brain.

BRENDA sits. ZIMMERMAN manages, from his sleeping bag, to get the bottle. He begins to drink it. BETH looks up from her A to Z.

BETH. Hey, Eddie —

EDDIE. Yuh?

BETH. You think we hit the wrong bughouse?

Enter HUGO and MARY from the stairs. MARY is in a nightie, clutching a blanket, a teddy bear, and the picture of St Theresa of Lisieux.

HUGO. Well, hallo, doctor.

EDDIE. Hugo, hey —

HUGO. You do know Mary?

EDDIE. Yes, we met —

HUGO. She's had a nasty dream.

Slight pause. BRENDA stands.

She's walking down the road. Sees men in berets, in a wire compound, and they're going to test the bomb. So down she goes, this passage, deep inside, where she'll be safe.

Slight pause.

But she's not safe, because she is the passage and the bomb's inside her. She has swallowed it, can't spew it up, or shit it out. It's going to explode.

Slight pause.

And so she wants to sleep, down, in the box, so it can melt away.

EDDIE. The box?

HUGO. It's Zimmerman's invention. Womb or tomb. For when you don't know if you're coming or going.

HUGO *takes* MARY *out left.*

EDDIE. Hey. We're right. We're here.

ZIMMERMAN (*still clutching the bottle, falling slowly back into the horizontal position*). There are no sins inside the gates of Eden.

BLACKOUT.

Scene Five

Faintly, we hear music: a Gregorian chant, behind which is the whimpering of a woman's voice. A spot fades up on HUGO. During the speech, a spot fades up on MARY, in the black box, lit up, clutching her teddy.

HUGO. Mary Barnes was born in 1923. She had a brother, Simon. School, she couldn't speak. Her mother took her to the doctor. College, she was trained to be a nurse. Her brother tried to touch her body and he was committed to a mental hospital. She was converted to Catholicism. Four years later, she was put in mental hospital. Padded cell. Discharged within a year. Returned to her career. But underneath it, all, still crazy.

Pause. MARY in the box.

In 1963, she moved into a hostel. But they couldn't cope. She was obsessed with masturbation. Priest said one thing, therapist another. We told her we were setting up a new community, but she'd have to wait a year until it opened. Many times, she nearly broke down, streets and public places, but she kept herself at bay. Until she came to live in the community.

Pause. MARY, in the box, falls gently over on to her side. She lies still.

She came to live in the community. She'd been told she must stay sane. One thing and then another. She was put in mental hospital. Became a Catholic. She saw her brother put in mental hospital. She grew up silent. She was born.

Pause. The lights fade on MARY.

Without her fingernails. Feet first. She couldn't suck. Her

mother's pain. No milk to give. The agony inside her. Like a bomb. The tearing pain.

BLACKOUT.

Scene Six

LIGHTS. *Main area. Day.* BETH *sits in an armchair, reading a book.* HUGO *and* DOUGLAS *enter from the stairs.*

DOUGLAS. Of course she thinks she's a foetus.

HUGO. No. She *is* a foetus. That's what she's experiencing.

DOUGLAS. OK, fine —

HUGO. And foetuses don't sort of eat.

Enter EDDIE *left with a clothes-line. His mouth is full of clothes-pegs. He attaches one end of the line to a hook on stage left, the other to a hook on the opposite side. He goes out. All this as:*

DOUGLAS. That's right. The problem is, she is also a 40-year-old woman. And if 40-year-old women don't sort of eat, they do have this tendency to sort of die of starvation. So she must be fed.

EDDIE re-enters with newspapers, which he starts spreading under the clothes-line. BRENDA *enters from the stairs with a basket of dirty washing. She crosses and out left.*

HUGO. She wants to be. *Be* fed. She doesn't want to *eat.*

Enter ZIMMERMAN *with a basket of clean washing. He dumps it and goes out. As:*

DOUGLAS. Oh, yes?

HUGO. She wants a stomach tube. Fed directly like a foetus.

DOUGLAS. Highly dangerous.

HUGO. It's difficult.

DOUGLAS. It's highly dangerous.

HUGO. Not highly.

Enter BRENDA *with another basket of clean washing.* BETH *puts down her book and starts to roll a joint of marijuana.*

DOUGLAS. And what happens if she dies?

EDDIE looks up. He's finished laying the newspaper. He stands

up. He starts to hang the washing from the left end, from
ZIMMERMAN's basket.

To us? To here? The medical authorities?

HUGO. Oh, of course, the —

DOUGLAS. Not to mention her?

BRENDA *takes clothes pegs from the top of her basket, and*
starts hanging from the other end. ZIMMERMAN
enters with more clothes pegs and starts hanging washing in
the middle.

BRENDA. She paints breasts on the wall. She wants the breast,
milk. Doesn't she? So all we've got to do is find some way, some
one, to give her milk. Yes? No?

HUGO. They're hardly pleasant breasts. They're painted with her
shit. They're horrid, smelly, shitty breasts. Not nice at all.

BRENDA. She thinks they're nice. She sculpts them into little
figures. Little shitty babies.

EDDIE (*mouth full of pegs*). Uf vads vo —

He spits out the pegs.

If that's so, then eating might have something to do with sex,
and so it's not surprising that she's fairly choosy about who
feeds her.

He and BRENDA carry on pegging. By now, BETH is obscured
from view behind the clothes line of washing.

DOUGLAS. Cos, after all, we're not a hospital.

HUGO. Well, OK, Duggie, fine, but we should still try the tubes,
cos if we don't, then the only choice, and I hope you don't
mean this, Duggie, only choice is that she goes, goes into a real
hospital, and gets her mind blown up with drugs and ECT.

DOUGLAS. Yes, as you say. We've come here to avoid the kind of
mental health that gets its kicks from putting things in people.

HUGO. Duggie. It's *her* voyage. *She* planned it. Somewhere in
there, under all the weeds and bricks and broken bottles, far
from the light, there's a little rugged seedling poking up its nose,
the only thing that's living, and if we don't stamp on it, there is
a chance that it'll grow again. Up straight, this time. Not with
our help. We leave it be. Just give it — life support. Now do you
see that, Duggie?

BRENDA. Um —

HUGO *and* DOUGLAS *turn to her.*

Um, you know my views. About the medical authorities.

Slight pause.

The purpose of most psychiatric practice is to cauterize
dissent.

Slight pause.

That's why we must protect ourselves, this place, from them.
So she must eat.

HUGO. Then someone has to tell her to. And hope she will. That's
all.

BRENDA. I'll tell her.

DOUGLAS. Good.

Exit DOUGLAS.

BRENDA. But I can't — she needs looking after, all of every day.

Pause.

EDDIE. I'll feed her.

HUGO. Wonderful. Thanks, Eddie.

Exit HUGO.

BRENDA (*to* EDDIE). Right.

She goes out to the stairs.

EDDIE. Um . . . what have I . . .

He goes out left. ZIMMERMAN *turns from the washing.*

ZIMMERMAN. Well I dunno. They come over here, take all the
houses, grab all the jobs, rape our women and abuse our
national assistance, and now they're trying to hijack our lunatics.
I dunno.

*He notices the washing is sagging heavily in the middle. He goes
and tries to pull the line tighter. It breaks and the washing falls
down.*

Shit.

BETH *has been revealed. She is sitting cross-legged on the
armchair, the book open on her lap, the lighted joint in her hand.*

BETH. Oh little creature, formed of joy and mirth;
Go, live without the help of anything on earth.

She offers the joint to ZIMMERMAN.

That's shit.

ZIMMERMAN *takes the joint.* BETH *gestures to the book on her lap.*

That's William Blake.

ZIMMERMAN *smokes the joint.* BLACKOUT.

Scene Seven

LIGHTS *on* MARY's *room.* MARY *lying on her mattress.* BRENDA *sits by her.*

BRENDA. Mary. Hey, Mary, do you want to eat?

MARY. Ugh, ugh.

BRENDA. Mary, you're going to have to eat.

MARY. The tubes.

BRENDA. Mary, we got to talk about the tubes.

MARY *sits up, looks at* BRENDA, *suddenly wide awake.*

Mary, everyone's worried, about your state of health.

MARY. Uh?

BRENDA. You haven't —

MARY (*harshly*). Tubes. TUBES. I want the TUBES, you bitch!

Shrieks with fury.

TUBES!

BRENDA (*calmly*). Mary, we haven't the facilities here to tube-feed you. This doesn't mean that this might not be right for you, but we can't do it, here, and we don't want you to die of malnutrition, so if you wish to stay in the community, then you must eat.

MARY *bursts into tears.*

Oh, Mary.

MARY. Wha've I done.

BRENDA. You haven't done anything.

MARY. Why you gone against yourself.

BRENDA. I haven't gone against myself.

MARY. You gone against my therapy. You're pun'shing me. I killed you. Wrong, wrong, wrong. I killed you.

BRENDA. Mary, look at me, you haven't killed me, Mary.

EDDIE comes in with a bottle of milk.

MARY (*to* BRENDA). Wrong, wrong, wrong.

EDDIE. Hey. Mary.

MARY. Eddie, Brenda wants to stop me going down.

EDDIE (*sits*). No, no-one wants to stop you going down.

MARY. Do, Eddie, do.

EDDIE. No, Mary. Nothing's wrong. It's not your fault. We just can't feed you through a tube.

MARY. I tried to kill her, Eddie.

EDDIE. Didn't, Mary. Look.

Pause. MARY sneaks a look at BRENDA. Pause. Then EDDIE sits, on the mattress, picks up the bottle.

EDDIE. Drink, now?

MARY. 'lright.

MARY starts to drink.

EDDIE. Nice?

MARY. Mm.

MARY drinks. Then EDDIE turns his head, slightly, to look at BRENDA, to acknowledge his pleasure that MARY is drinking. This small gesture causes MARY to feel very bad, and she spits the milk out, in EDDIE's face.

MARY. Wrong. WRONG, Eddie!

EDDIE himself takes a drink of the bottle, and spits it over MARY. MARY looks astonished. Then EDDIE gives the bottle to MARY, who drinks and spits over EDDIE. She begins to chuckle. EDDIE drinks and spits. MARY drinks and spits. Laughs. EDDIE takes the bottle, drinks and swallows.

EDDIE. Glug-ug-ug.

MARY looks at him. He drinks again.

Glug-ug-ug-ug.

MARY laughs, she takes the bottle, drinks.

MARY. Glug-ug-ug-ug.

EDDIE (*takes the bottle, drinks*). Glug-ug-ug-ug.

MARY (*takes the bottle, drinks*). Glug-ug-ug-ug.

> *She takes the bottle from her lips.* EDDIE *doesn't take it back.*
> *She chuckles, repeats the noise.*

> Glug-ug.

EDDIE. Come on, you want to finish up?

MARY. Mm mm.

> *He cradles her in his arms and feeds her with the bottle.*
> BRENDA *stands.*

BRENDA. Night Mary.

MARY (*whispered, through the drinking*). Night.

BRENDA. See you in the morning.

> *Exit* BRENDA. MARY *drinks.*

EDDIE. That's right. Drink it up.

> MARY *drinks, finishes.*

> All gone? All gone.

MARY. Mm.

> *Pause.* EDDIE, *very gently.*

> Hey. Knock, knock. Who's there?

MARY. It's Mary.

EDDIE. Mary who?

> MARY *doesn't reply. Pause. Then* EDDIE *leaves her. Stands,*
> *goes to the door. Suddenly,* MARY, *furious, turns and shrieks*
> *at him.*

MARY. Why are you so angry with me, Eddie?

EDDIE. Me?

> BLACKOUT.

Scene Eight

LIGHTS *on the main area. Morning.* DOUGLAS *sits reading,*
drinking coffee and smoking a cigarette. EDDIE's *voice, offstage,*
singing raucously.

EDDIE.   Little Miss Muffet
            Sat on a tuffet
            Eating her curds and whey

Enter EDDIE *left.*

> A nasty great spider
> Sat down beside her
> And . . . Mm?

DOUGLAS. Frightened Miss Muffet away.

EDDIE (*sings, as he goes out to stairs*). And frightened Miss Muffet away . . .

> MARY's *room. She lies asleep, on her mattress.* HALF-LIGHT *downstairs. During the following,* BETH *enters with a duster, a drying-up cloth and a tray of cutlery. She puts the tray on the chair.* DOUGLAS *nods to her and goes out. She dusts the table. And, from off, other noises of the day: a radio somewhere, a hoover.* EDDIE *comes into* MARY's *room. He takes from his pocket a big black rubber spider on an elastic string. He dangles it over* MARY.

EDDIE. Look what I got you, Mary.

MARY (*waking*). Uh . . . uh?

EDDIE. Spider, Mary.

MARY. Oh, Eddie.

EDDIE. Great big spider, come to get you.

MARY (*grabbing the spider*). Oh, EDDIE.

EDDIE. Hey, d'you want to get up?

> MARY *is playing with the spider and making little noises at it.*

Come on, get up, race you down the stairs.

MARY. What? Oh, yes.

> *She jumps out of bed.* EDDIE *finding her clothes, tossing them to her.*

EDDIE. Come on, let's go . . .

MARY (*desperately flinging her clothes on*). Oh, Eddie, coming, don't go, just a minute —

EDDIE. Hey, Mary, you not ready yet?

MARY. Oh, just a minute, Eddie, nearly ready —

EDDIE (*helping* MARY, *who's having problems with her jumper*). Come on, arms up, that's it.

> MARY's *ready.*

OK?

Suddenly, EDDIE *running out of the room followed by* MARY.
LIGHTS *full downstairs, out upstairs.* EDDIE *into main area,
and down behind the table, 'shhhing' at* BETH, *who follows
events in this sequence with ironic detachment.* MARY, *who's
entered, looks around. At* BETH, BETH *shrugs.*

MARY. Eddie. Eddie. Where are you, Eddie?

She senses EDDIE's *somewhere round the table, goes round one
side, as he crawls round the other. Then the other way round.
Then she goes down on all fours.*

Where — are — you?

EDDIE *growls, appears under the table.* BETH *still trying to
dust.*

EDDIE. Hey, what's that? What's there?

He growls. MARY *growls.*

Is it a bear? Is it a tiger?

EDDIE *and* MARY *circling each other on all fours.*

MARY. It's a — crocodile.

MARY *bites* EDDIE. EDDIE *bites* MARY. *They make
crocodile noises at each other. During the following, at a distance,
a phone rings, merging into the other domestic noises. Half a
dozen rings, then stops.*

EDDIE. Hey, is that all your mouth is?

MARY. Mary's got the biggest mouth.

EDDIE. No she hasn't. Eddie has.

He opens his mouth wide.

MARY (*opening her mouth very wide*). 'o 'ary 'as.

She puts her finger in her mouth to demonstrate.

'ook, 'ook, 'ary 'as.

Growling, EDDIE's *fingers approach* MARY's *mouth. He puts
his fingers in her mouth. Withdraws.*

EDDIE. OK, so Mary's got the biggest mouth. But who's got the
sharpest teeth?

EDDIE *bites* MARY. MARY *bites* EDDIE. *Both growling,*
MARY *is squealing with delight.* EDDIE *grabs a chair, still
kneeling, growling through the bars.* MARY *does the same with
another chair. Enter* BRENDA.

BRENDA. Eddie, it's the London School of Economics, on the telephone.

She goes out. BETH *starts to lay the table, polishing the cutlery with the cloth as she does so.*

EDDIE. OK, croc. You stay there, and I'll be right back.

MARY *growls,* EDDIE *getting up.*

That's right. You stay right there, in the river. Won't be a minute.

EDDIE *goes out.* MARY *growls. Then again, a little uncertain. Then,* BETH *looking at her, a little growl at* BETH. BETH *smiles.* MARY *is still.*

BETH. Hey, Mary, you want to help me lay the table?

MARY *goes rigid, clutching the chair.* BETH *takes a step towards her.*

Mm?

Another step.

Want to help me lay the knives out?

Pause. MARY *still rigid.*

OK.

BETH *turns back to the table,* MARY *throws the chair at her.*

MARY (*as she throws*). Can't go! I mustn't go away!

BETH. Oh, for Christ's sake, Mary —

Re-enter EDDIE.

Eddie, that woman just threw this chair at me.

EDDIE (*rushes to* MARY, *who's lying rigid*). Hey, what's up, Mary?

BETH. Hey, what's up, Beth? I just had a chair thrown at me.

MARY. Came in. Came in on me.

EDDIE. It's OK, Mary.

BETH. Well, it may be OK Mary —

MARY. Broken, Eddie.

BETH. She was doing the chair-tossing.

MARY. Felt splintered, exploding, Eddie —

EDDIE. Yuh.

BETH. I mean, don't get me wrong, I'm really pleased to be a part of —

EDDIE. Beth.

> BETH *looks at* EDDIE *a moment. Then carries on laying the table.* EDDIE *to* MARY.

It's cos I went away. And you were jealous. Threw the chair cos she was coming in on you. You felt possessed. That made you angry.

MARY (*whispers*). No. Not angry, with you, Eddie.

> *Exit* BETH.

EDDIE. Yuh, Mary, you were angry with me.

MARY (*whispers*). No, no.

> *Getting angry.*

No, you know I'd not be angry with you, Eddie!

EDDIE. Mary, you *look* angry now.

MARY (*hits* EDDIE *on the chest*). No! No! No! Confuse me. No, not angry, Eddie!

EDDIE. Hey, is that all you can hit, Mary?

MARY (*hits* EDDIE). No! No! No!

EDDIE. Hey, I bet you can hit me more than that.

MARY (*grunting as she hits* EDDIE). Uh. Uh. Uh. Uh. Uh.

> *And she grabs him round the middle.*

EDDIE. Hey? What's this now?

MARY. Snake.

EDDIE. Snake? Squeezing me?

MARY. Yuh. Squeezy-snake.

EDDIE. Hey, is that all you can squeeze? Snakey? Is that all?

> MARY *squeezes as tight as she can. Then, finally, she lets go, falls back, panting, exhausted, happy.* EDDIE *breathless as well. Then he turns to* MARY.

Mary. You bit my ear. You hit me. Yuh? And I'm still here. And I bit you. And you're fine. Anger doesn't hurt me, and it doesn't kill you either. Both OK.

> *Pause.* EDDIE *looks round. Sees the drying-up cloth. Quickly, he reaches for it, takes it, and covers* MARY's *head with it.*

MARY (*under the cloth*). Uh?

EDDIE. Hey, where's Mary Barnes?

MARY. Uh?

EDDIE. She's gone away, she's all gone away.

He stands, looks round the room.

Hey! Where's Mary? Is she gone?

MARY *pulls off the cloth, appears, grinning.*

Oh, *there* she is.

MARY *grins, puts the cloth back over her face.*

Hey, now she's gone again.

MARY *reappears.*

Nope, she's there.

MARY *puts the cloth over her face.*

Nope, she's gone.

MARY *still.*

Still gone.

MARY *still.*

Well, there we are. No Mary, any more.

Slowly, MARY *pulls the cloth off her face.*

Well. If it isn't Mary Barnes.

Pause.

See. She can go. And she comes back again. And Eddie, goes, and Eddie comes right back again.

He puts his finger in her mouth, and then takes it out.

And Eddie comes in Mary, and she isn't hurt; and Eddie goes out, and she isn't hurt.

Pause. HUGO *has appeared. Stands there.*

And the spider's outside you, Mary.

Pause.

HUGO. Mary, Mary, Quite contrary.
How does your garden grow.

EDDIE. Slowly.

BLACKOUT.

Scene Nine

Main area. The COMMUNITY *is eating dinner.* EDDIE *sits between* MARY *and* BETH.

DOUGLAS. Apparently, some German doctors diagnose a schizophrenic on the basis of a feeling they get within themselves. The Praecox Feeling.

Slight pause.

Man who's threatened. Says he's petrified. That's fine. The man who says that he's a stone, is liable to get locked up. To petrify means that: to turn to stone.

Slight pause.

One might define 'delusion' as a real idea a person holds, but which a psychiatrist deludes himself into taking literally.

ZIMMERMAN. A shrink once put his patient on a lie-detector test, and asked the question: Are you Jesus Christ? The lie-detector registered he hadn't told the truth. He'd answered 'no'.

BETH. My father is a businessman. My mother's father was a building worker. Wanted me to go to college, be an architect. I couldn't draw. Dropped out. Just sat around. They shouted at me. World of my own, they said. So took me to a doctor. Couldn't move. He said that I was catatonic.

EDDIE. Scared. Scared stiff.

MARY. Eddie, why so cold?

EDDIE. It is. The central heating's playing up.

MARY. Oh, Eddie, wha've I done.

MARY. You haven't. Not your fault. You don't control the central heating. It's a thing.

MARY. Oh, Eddie.

EDDIE. Come on, eat your food.

DOUGLAS. Can I give anyone some more?

Pause as he hands round seconds.

BRENDA. The very word is *in*valid. Invalid. You know, in feudal times, there were no mad, or sane, defined as such. Communities supported those who couldn't work, quite automatically. But then, when people started being paid in cash, as individual workers, then the criminal, the ill, the lunatic, were separated off. Defined as 'other'. On the grounds of being unexploitable. Their *functioning* impaired.

HUGO. The mad in England are defined as cured when capable of work.

BRENDA. It's even more. The roles of family fixed roles as father, mother, daughter, son, are products of commodity production. People, defined by their relations to commodities. I own, therefore I am. You are, the things you buy.

EDDIE. Last century, the Southern States, the medical profession had to classify a new disease. Occurred exclusively among black slaves. They called it drapetomania. It was manifested in the slave's desire to run away.

BETH. My parents were religious. Didn't let me stay out late or wear cosmetics. Father spoke a lot about not lying, being honest. Used to falsify his tax returns. Deceive competitors. He said so. Couldn't make it fit. I told them, once, I want to go with men. I was beside myself. I didn't mean it. Said it wasn't me.

EDDIE. They meant, you were possessed.

MARY. Oh, Eddie.

EDDIE. Yuh?

MARY. That salt. Salt on your food.

EDDIE. I like it.

MARY. Why you punishing yourself.

EDDIE. I'm not. Like salt. You don't.

MARY. Why punish me?

Slight pause. BETH *stands and goes out left.*

DOUGLAS. The issue, surely, is authority.

BRENDA. The issue's state authority.

HUGO. Not all authority?

EDDIE. The issue's violence.

BRENDA. The issue is state violence.

HUGO. All violence?

EDDIE. The violence of people to each other.

DOUGLAS. In each other. Cop that really matters is the cop inside your head.

BRENDA. The cop that really matters is the cop that's in the streets.

ZIMMERMAN. The revolution's fucking in the road.

BRENDA. The revolution is not fucking in the road.

HUGO. The revolution . . . Is just saying what we mean.

DOUGLAS. Who isn't?

HUGO. None of you.

BETH *enters with pudding.*

BETH. Hey, pudding, anyone?

EDDIE. Hey, Mary, jelly?

MARY. No, not jelly.

EDDIE. Cheese?

MARY. Eddie, it seems wrong to eat.

EDDIE. OK.

MARY. But seems wrong not to eat. I feel so bad.

EDDIE. You're angry, cos I'm talking to the others, Mary, cos I been with you all day. OK?

MARY. OK.

EDDIE *turns to* BETH.

BETH. Also, I had this brother —

MARY. Whore.

Slight pause.

EDDIE. Beth, ignore her, she's just mad with me.

MARY. You whore.

EDDIE. It's OK, she doesn't mean it.

MARY. Whore.

EDDIE. Just saying that, cos she's so —

MARY. WHORE.

BETH *stands, goes to the record player, puts on a record: Hey Mr Tambourine Man by the Byrds.*

MARY. WHORE.

BETH *turns up the volume.*

WHORE.

BETH *turns up the volume.*

WHORE.

BETH (*turns and screams at* MARY). WHAT HAVE I DONE TO YOU?

A crash from off left. DOUGLAS *to the record player, turns it off. Crash, from the other side. Exit* DOUGLAS *and* BRENDA *left*, HUGO *right.*

MARY. Uh –

EDDIE (*quickly stands*). Come on, Mary.

MARY (*as she is gets to her feet*). Uh, Joe, me –

EDDIE. Not you, Mary. Come on, bed.

He takes MARY *out to the stairs. She's moaning. Re-enter* BRENDA.

BRENDA. They're smashing windows, all around.

ZIMMERMAN. Who?

BRENDA. How do I know? Put shit, through the letterbox.

BETH. What?

BRENDA. Shit. Splat.

Enter HUGO.

HUGO. Can't see anyone. I heard them shouting, nutters, perverts, layabouts.

ZIMMERMAN. Who?

HUGO (*quietly*). The working class. With Morris Minors, television sets. Sucked in.

BRENDA (*angry*). Sucked in to what?

HUGO. Sucked into nutters, perverts, layabouts.

Slight pause.

ZIMMERMAN. Three people. One says he's Marx, and with enough to follow him, he'll change the world. Another says he's Jesus Christ, and with enough to follow him, he'll change the world. The third, who is a doctor of psychiatry, he thinks he'll change the world all on his own. So which of them's the most deranged, then think ye?

Enter DOUGLAS.

DOUGLAS. I've just called the police.

BRENDA. You've what?

DOUGLAS. You heard.

ZIMMERMAN. Out of whose head?

Another crash and BLACKOUT. *In the darkness, the Beatles'*
Why Don't We Do It In The Road.

Scene Ten

Early morning. Main area. HUGO *sits.* DOUGLAS *and* BRENDA
stand. ZIMMERMAN *lies on the table, amid the debris.* KEITH
stands stage left.

KEITH. They, see . . . I mean, they're up at six or half past, lots of
them. Your bedtime, just before them getting up.

Slight pause.

I mean, it is, they're not that keen. Asylum, in the street. Can
understand. Your, style of life.

Slight pause.

I'm sorry. Got to get to work.

Exit KEITH. *Pause.*

ZIMMERMAN. Outside, above those rows of leggo houses, there's
a great fat grinning greasy fried egg of a sun.

He sits up.

They're soapboxes. They let the wind in. Only thing to do, is
stand on them and shout.

HUGO. They don't.

DOUGLAS. Perhaps they're frightened they'll fall off.

HUGO. The vertigo of freedom.

Pause.

Minute to minute. White rabbits. Need to stop the ticking,
listen to the heartbeat.

Slight pause.

Dali only melted clocks. We need to wrench their precious
little coggy innards out, and stop them telling us their time.

ZIMMERMAN *finds a bottle, pours a drink.*

Who else? But mad psychiatrists. And lunatics and layabouts
and perverts. And where else but here. Are we to find our
timeless time?

ZIMMERMAN (*drinks*). It's enough to drive you sane.

BLACKOUT *and another burst of Why Don't We Do It In The Road.*

Scene Eleven

Immediately, in the DARKNESS.

MARY. Eddie! No, Eddie! No, no, no . . .

LIGHTS. *Main area.* EDDIE *enters, from the stairs, in a suit. He carries a briefcase, and is drinking a cup of coffee, and he's late. He puts down the cup as enter* MARY *behind him.*

MARY. No, Eddie —

EDDIE. Mary, I told you. I am going to the Clinic. For three hours. I'll be back.

He turns to go. MARY *grabs him round the middle.*

MARY. No, no, Eddie. You don't mean it.

EDDIE (*pulling himself free*). Mary, I do mean it, I am going out, I'm late.

MARY (*grabbing him again*). Wha've I done. Oh, wha've I done.

EDDIE (*pulling himself free again*). Mary, stop it.

MARY *whines.*

Mary, stop that noise.

MARY *drops to the floor, whining.*

Mary, I am going to the clinic, now.

He turns to go.

MARY. Eddie?

EDDIE (*turns back*). Yes?

MARY. Eddie, must tell you . . .

EDDIE. Come on, spit it out.

MARY. That if you go 'way, I'll run into the street, tear off my clothes, and scream out Take Me To A Mental Hospital.

EDDIE *shuts his eyes.*

EDDIE. What?

MARY. You heard me.

EDDIE *takes a decision. He turns to go.* MARY *to her feet, rushes, grabs him, pulls him round, screams.*

MARY. TAKE ME TO A MENTAL —

    EDDIE punches MARY in the face. She staggers back.

EDDIE. Oh, no.

    MARY's hands go to her face.

    Oh, Mary, why do you make me . . .

    MARY's hands are covered in blood from her bleeding nose.

    Oh Christ.

MARY. Blood. My blood.

    She turns round.

EDDIE. Hey, now, Mary . . .

MARY. Hugo! Brenda! Duggie! Look, my blood!

    She runs out up the stairs.

EDDIE. Mary —

    BETH enters from the kitchen, eating a bowl of cornflakes.

BETH. What?

EDDIE. Hit Mary.

BETH. Oh. Hit Mary.

    She wanders across.

EDDIE. Hit my patient.

BETH. Eddie.

    Taps her head.

    Doc inside your head.

    She goes out right as DOUGLAS enters from the stairs.

EDDIE. Duggie, I —

DOUGLAS. I know. She seems delighted.

EDDIE. What?

DOUGLAS. She says you brought her badness out. Her badness, bomb, all down her nose it came.

    Pause. EDDIE to the stairs, shouts up.

EDDIE. Knock knock! Who's there?

MARY (*off*). It's Mary!

EDDIE. Mary who?

Pause. EDDIE *turns back.*

Oh, sure, delighted.

He looks at his watch. He shakes his head in fury, goes out left. Then BLACKOUT *downstairs and* LIGHTS *on* MARY's *room. She sits on her mattress, blood pouring down her face.*

MARY. This is my body. This is my blood. This is Mary Barnes.

BLACKOUT.

Act Two

Scene One

The main area. EDDIE enters one side, with a flat, round tin.
MARY the other.

EDDIE. Mary.

MARY. Eddie.

EDDIE. Present for you.

MARY. What?

>   *He tosses her the tin. She catches it, opens it. It's full of crayons.*
>   *Eddie.*

EDDIE. Crayons.

MARY. Oh . . .

EDDIE. No need to paint with shit. No need to smear on walls.

MARY. Oh . . .

EDDIE. Now, go on. Draw.

>   BLACKOUT.

Scene Two

Main area. On a chair, MARY's drawing crayons, brushes, pots of
paint, cloths and so on.
>   *LAURENCE, a man in his late 30s, sits at the record player. He*
>   *is watching a record go round on the turntable. A few moments.*
>   *Then he puts the record on. It's Paint it Black by the Rolling*
>   *Stones, but we only hear the intro, for LAURENCE takes off the*
>   *needle just before the lyrics start. He watches the record going*
>   *round again, then puts on the needle again, takes it off at the end*
>   *of the intro once again. He watches the record going round.*
>   *Enter HUGO right, followed by BRENDA.*

BRENDA. Hugo, are you shopping?

HUGO. Shopping? No. Why?

BRENDA. Because it's your turn. There's no food in the house. The
  only thing in the kitchen is a cluster of thirty dirty milk-bottles
  and while you're out you might return them.

HUGO. Thursday. Zimmerman's turn.

BRENDA. I don't know where he is. I think he's gone.

HUGO. Gone? Why?

Enter MARY carrying a rolled-up canvas.

BRENDA. Dunno. Perhaps we disagreed with him.

HUGO. Can't you . . . Oh, all right.

HUGO *goes out left.*

MARY (*to BRENDA, explaining the painting*). The Temptations of Christ. The Devil comes on, horrible, cos God made him come bad. But now the temple, gold. The mountain, every colour. Christ is silver, cool.

BRENDA *smiles at MARY.*

I'll hang it up.

MARY *goes out right. LAURENCE puts on the record again. The same ritual, playing the intro twice. BRENDA looks on. LAURENCE takes off the needle, watches the record going round. Enter DOUGLAS with a piece of paper.*

DOUGLAS. Brenda, what is this?

He gives her the paper.

BRENDA. I don't know. It's a group of artists. They want to stage an event.

DOUGLAS. Brenda, I'm a bit concerned —

BRENDA. Mm?

DOUGLAS. That we're being kind of taken over —

BRENDA. Well —

DOUGLAS. By freaks, and you know —

BRENDA. Freaks?

DOUGLAS *takes the paper back.*

DOUGLAS. I mean.

He reads, as MARY enters with a painting on hardboard.

"Eeeevent. We shall stop show stop bits of people cut off cut up cut together question mark. The porpoise only is relieved in T.I.M.E. stop. England E.S.P. ects that every man will groove his beauty, and achieve a state of stroke ultimate hydraulic maya that maybe semi-colon. Please bring offall dash."

It's very hard to follow. It's erratically punctuated. I am not 100 percent convinced, in fact, that it means anything at all.

BRENDA *shrugs, exit.*

MARY (*to* DOUGLAS, *explaining the painting*). Disintegration. Devil's clawing bits of people he has broken, but he can't engulf them, cos St Michael spears his heart.

DOUGLAS *smiles at* MARY.

I'll nail it up.

Exit MARY. DOUGLAS *sits.* LAURENCE *repeats his ritual with the record. Enter* HUGO *left carrying a large number of empty milk bottles.*

DOUGLAS (*stands*). Ah, Hugo —

HUGO *drops one of the milk bottles. It smashes. Pause.*

HUGO. Did you know that people's bodies, in America, are so irradiated, that it's illegal to transport mother's milk across state lines? Except, of course, in the original containers.

DOUGLAS. No, I didn't know that.

Pause. HUGO *indicates he can't do anything about the bottle he's smashed without risking dropping the others.* DOUGLAS *goes out. Enter* MARY *with another painting.* DOUGLAS *re-enters with a dustpan and brush, sweeps up the broken bottle, as* MARY *explains her painting to* HUGO.

MARY. God's Mother. 'Fore the world, bordered in gold. The breasts are revealed. They succour men.

HUGO *smiles, goes out.*

I'll put it in the Games Room.

Exit MARY. *Exit* DOUGLAS *with the dustpan.* LAURENCE *goes and upends the chair with* MARY's *things. He sits on the chair.* MARY *re-enters.*

MARY. Laurence.

LAURENCE. Yes.

MARY. My chair.

LAURENCE. It is.

MARY. My things.

LAURENCE. They are.

MARY. Laurence, get off my chair.

LAURENCE. Gimme a reason.

MARY. No!

LAURENCE. Then no.

> MARY *attacks* LAURENCE. *They fight, rolling across the floor, like children, having fun, shouting and biting, knocking over chairs.* BRENDA, DOUGLAS *and* BETH *enter.* MARY *and* LAURENCE *become aware of their presence, stop fighting.*

BETH. What a shit-heap.

BRENDA. Yes. Laurence, Mary, you must tidy up.

> MARY *and* LAURENCE *stand up sheepishly.*

BETH. All these things.

BRENDA. Yes. Mary, you must move your things.

MARY. Don't —

BRENDA. What?

MARY. Don't boss me.

BRENDA. Other people keep things in their room.

MARY. Don't tell me what to do.

BRENDA (*picks up a chair*). Now, come on, Mary love, let's get this —

MARY. Do what EDDIE says.

DOUGLAS (*sits*). Yes. Eddie

> *Pause.* MARY *knocks over a chair.* LAURENCE *picks it up. Picks up another.* MARY *knocks over another chair.* LAURENCE *sits at the record player, watches the record go round. Pause. A door slam, left.* EDDIE, *briskly, comes in left, throws a cardboard file on the table, sits, puts his feet up. He looks at the* OTHERS *and then explains.*

EDDIE. I have just been to a committee meeting of an organization of radical therapists entitled Shrinks for Socialism.

> *Slight pause.*

They are planning a conference on the Gestalt Road to Revolution that will form, I gather, the first step in a plan to take over the world on strict Marxist-Jungian lines. In the land of the mind, the slogan runs, the One-Id man is King.

> *Slight pause.*

Sadly, we didn't get that far. We were only, in fact, on Matters Arising when the Treasurer accused the Chairman of a conscious strategy of maternal double-bind and thereupon freaked out. She's very highly strung, I was informed. She should be, I replied.

Slight pause. To BETH, *grossly.*

Hey, Beth, why not just lie down and do the first thing that comes into my head?

Pause. Senses the atmosphere, stands.

Well, then, I'll just go and —

MARY. Eddie.

EDDIE. Hallo, Mary. How's your day.

MARY. Eddie, please tell them.

EDDIE. Tell them what?

MARY. About the Games Room.

EDDIE. Oh, the Games Room.

Pause. Looking at the OTHERS.

Now?

MARY. Yes, now.

Pause.

DOUGLAS. Well?

EDDIE. Uh, well. Mary wants to paint the Games Room. If that, meets with —

BRENDA. In the Games Room?

EDDIE. More like, on it. S'wall. A kind of — mural. Painting. On the wall.

Pause.

DOUGLAS. Last week, I remember, she did just that. With chalk. All over, walls and chairs, the billiard table. Criss-cross spider's web all over. Quite a mess.

EDDIE. She cleaned it up.

BRENDA. You cleaned it up.

Enter HUGO *left, unnoticed, with bags of shopping.*

EDDIE. Connections. Everyone connected to each other.

BETH. What?

EDDIE. That's what she meant.

Pause.

DOUGLAS. There is an awful lot of Mary Barnes around this house. It is, in fact, quite difficult, avoiding it.

HUGO. Right. Bread and wine. I shall, at last, make supper.

Exit HUGO left. MARY, quite suddenly.

MARY. My mother said — don't paint outside the lines. I sploshed about, I shouldn't paint outside the lines. My mother was a spider. You are like a Mother to me, Brenda.

LAURENCE *puts on his Stones record. He lets it run.*
BLACKOUT *and it covers the change.*

Scene Three

Dinner. The COMMUNITY, except for ZIMMERMAN, sit round the table. The evocations of the tableau rather stronger than before.

HUGO. A story. Backward of a Glasgow bughouse. Jockie lies there, screaming, getaway ya buggers, getaway. To quieten him, the surgeon decides to perform a transorbital lobotomy. And it's a great success, for after it, old Jockie is heard screaming, Canna hear the buggas, canna hear the buggas now no more.

DOUGLAS. Well, that's most affecting. Anyone here in favour of transorbital lobotomies?

HUGO. Another story. Woman had a phobia about Group Therapy. For which, she'd been prescribed. The day it came, she tried to run away. They rugby-tackled her, injected tranquillizer, dragged her to the room. And if they hadn't, so the doctor said, she would have missed her therapy.

DOUGLAS. That's very salutory. Wonder if there's anybody here would want to do that kind of thing?

EDDIE. It isn't mad to want to paint on walls. Leonardo painted things on walls.

DOUGLAS. Oh, Jesus.

HUGO. You mustn't talk to yourself, Duggie. You'll get locked up in mental hospital.

BRENDA. Anyone? Some wine?

BRENDA *pours wine.*

Mary, love, eat.

MARY *still.*

BETH. You don't eat up, you won't get your dessert.

EDDIE. Leave her alone.

BETH. Well, should she? Laurence eats all of his.

EDDIE. Well, Laurence isn't —

MARY *suddenly starts eating, very quickly.*

LAURENCE. S'good for you. The greens.

DOUGLAS. All right. Shall we stop pretending?

HUGO. Yes, let's stop pretending. Stop pretending what?

DOUGLAS. Well, for a start, let's drop this crap about no rules.

HUGO. Go on.

DOUGLAS. I will. Rule one. There are no rules. Rule two. It is against the rules to question rule one. Rule three. It is against the rules to acknowledge the existence of rules one and two.

BRENDA. What are you suggesting, Duggie?

DOUGLAS. I'm suggesting that we are pretending not to have rules, and we should admit that we have rules, and people who break them persistently should leave the community. I am suggesting that we are pretending not to be doctors and we are doctors and we can in the context of a non-coercive environment, without drugs or shocks, admit to so being. I am suggesting that the community is falling apart because of its childlike faith that if you scatter sick seed on the ground and neither prune nor tend nor water it then by a process of immaculate semination it will mend and heal and grow.

BRENDA. What are you suggesting.

DOUGLAS. A medical director of the community. Rules on admittance and dismissal from the community. Regular, compulsory meetings of the community to discuss —

HUGO. When you say dismissal, did you have anyone in mind?

DOUGLAS *cuts a piece of bread.* MARY *is making terrible noises.*

DOUGLAS. You said it.

He hands the piece of bread to HUGO.

HUGO. No thank you. Anyone want a piece of bread?

No-one answers. With some grace, HUGO stands and collects the plates.

BRENDA. Mary, don't gobble.

MARY. Uh?

BETH. That awful noise.

Slight pause. MARY finishes her last mouthful, quietly.

HUGO (*collecting the plates*). You finished, Laurence?

LAURENCE. Yuh. Don't want no more.

MARY looks up as HUGO takes LAURENCE's half-eaten plateful of food. MARY hands her empty plate to HUGO pointedly. HUGO goes out, re-enters during:

EDDIE. I was once in a hospital in Los Angeles, where they had a ward, a dehierarchised ward, you know, own clothes and get up when you want, and every day they had this group discussion. And there was this girl, this pretty Puerto Rican girl. And one day, at group discussion, she was standing, swaying gently to the rhythm of the voices, when the Chief Psychiatrist made a reference to her, her case, her mental state. And she heared this, or anyway, reacted to it, cos she suddenly began to dance, dance with a deal of energy, and grace, that, well, lit up that dusty, sweaty room. And everyone, the patients and the nurses, just sat back, enjoyed the show. And no harm done, of course, no harm to anyone. And then the Chief Psychiatrist said, Miss Rivera, you're disturbing us, the meeting, would you please sit down. She didn't listen. Miss Rivera, don't you hear us? We, the meeting, are asking you to stop. She didn't seem to hear. Look, Miss Rivera, if you don't sit down, the group is going to send you to your room. And still she kept on dancing. So the Chief Psychiatrist called up two aides and said, the group's decided Miss Rivera mustn't be allowed to carry on disrupting our discussion. Will you please escort her to her room. They did. She put up quite a fight.

Pause. He looks at DOUGLAS.

Nothing succeeds like duress.

DOUGLAS. Eddie, would you like some cheese?

HUGO (*translates*). Eddie, shut up.

DOUGLAS. That was a very interesting story.

HUGO (*translates*). That wasn't a very relevant story.

DOUGLAS. Do tell me, what was your reaction? Did you clout him one?

EDDIE. Duggie, you're getting ever so slightly right up my nose —

DOUGLAS. Oh, come on, now, you're only saying that.

HUGO. You know, the only conceivable explanation of the Passion Story is that Judas thought there'd been some ghastly theological mistake, and he was the Messiah. Which, I'm sure, was quite an understandable delusion. Happens all the time.

Pleasantly, to DOUGLAS.

Another piece of bread?

EDDIE. Mary, want cheese?

MARY. No, no.

EDDIE. OK.

LAURENCE. That's cos you gobbled.

BRENDA. Beth, some cheese?

BETH *shakes her head.*

Laurence?

LAURENCE. Please.

MARY. Hey.

BRENDA. What?

MARY. He didn't finish.

BRENDA. Don't be silly, Mary.

MARY. Don't be silly? Don't be silly? Didn't finish.

EDDIE. Actually, in fact, she's right.

BRENDA. Oh, Eddie, please. Encourage them..

MARY. Laurence didn't finish. Didn't *finish*.

BRENDA. All right. Laurence didn't finish.

Pause. Hiatus.

DOUGLAS. It is, of course, for everyone. But it's principally for the sake of people going down. Who need support. Need structure and security. Need to be clear.

HUGO. So give me rules. Make me feel cosy.

DOUGLAS. Hugo, please.

HUGO. Behold, I have set before thee an open door, and no man can shut it. No, however much you're terrified of what's beyond.

DOUGLAS (*to* BRENDA). What do you think?

BRENDA *shrugs.*

HUGO (*to* BRENDA). What do you think.

BRENDA. I think this house is getting quite unpleasant as a place to live in. And I think I'll go and make some coffee.

She stands.

HUGO. No do *not* go and make some coffee.

BRENDA (*sits*). And I think I won't go and make some coffee.

DOUGLAS. Rule four. That Brenda is allowed not to react to me. Rule Five. That Brenda is not allowed, however, to ignore Hugo. Rule Six —

HUGO. Duggie, just tell me, what can I do to make you really loath me?

DOUGLAS. Um . . . Can I have notice of that question?

BRENDA (*stands*). COFFEE.

Slight pause.

Laurence, could you give me —

MARY (*suddenly, violently*). Laurence takes people's letters hides them. Peed in the Games Room. Put blood on my painting. Don't keep rules. Don't finish. Simon he said bloody had to have his mouth washed out with soap and water —

BETH. Who the fuck's Simon?

MARY (*stands*). Paintings must *stay up.* They're mine.

LAURENCE *stands. He's shaking. He goes out quickly.*

EDDIE. Sit down, Mary. Please.

MARY *throws herself into her chair.* DOUGLAS *smiling, playing with a fork.*

Duggie, you crow once more, you crow one time too often.

DOUGLAS. Now what have I done?

Pause.

BRENDA. Um . . . Shouldn't someone see what . . .

She's going out when LAURENCE *comes back in. He has a number of canvasses, pieces of paper, hardboards. He's taken them down. He drops them on the floor.* BRENDA *sits.*

LAURENCE. They said, the people said the paintings should come down. Douglas and everyone.

Slight pause.

You got inside me. Hurt my head. Made it my fault that you're ill.

MARY *throws herself at* LAURENCE. *She hits him, bites him.* HUGO *and* EDDIE *pulling her off.*

MARY. Betraying me. You are betraying me.

HUGO. Come on, love —

MARY. Denying me. You are denying me.

EDDIE. Mary, get off him —

MARY *is pulled off,* HUGO *sits,* EDDIE *lets her go. She runs to the table, throws a loaf of bread at* DOUGLAS *and a glass of wine at* HUGO.

MARY. THIS is my body. THIS is my blood. You're betraying me.

She stands there, shaking with fury.

DOUGLAS. Well. That is exactly what I mean. We have to talk about the future of this house.

BETH. Think she should go. She screams at people. Think she should go.

HUGO *is wiping the wine off his hands with a cloth.*

DOUGLAS. We've got to sort this out.

MARY *rushes off right, up the stairs.* EDDIE *stands to follow her.*

LAURENCE. You said they should come down.

DOUGLAS. No, Eddie, no.

EDDIE *turns back.*

If you want Mary, take her, live with her, and have your house covered in her paintings and her shit and have her scream at you, assault you, and that's fine. Or give her rules, and keep her in control, and keep her here, and that too is all fine. But she is taking over;

EDDIE. Well, that's great. You haven't got a cop inside your head. You got a whole division.

Pause.

DOUGLAS. Well. Now, I think I'm going to the pub.

He stands.

I think, that is in order. Anyone —

BETH. So'm I.

She stands.

HUGO (*slowly gets up*). Why not.

DOUGLAS. Um, Laurence, want to —

LAURENCE. I'm all right.

Slight pause.

You said they should come down.

He goes out right to the stairs.

DOUGLAS. Right, then.

To EDDIE.

They're on me.

DOUGLAS *and* BETH *go out. As* HUGO *follows them.*

EDDIE. Hey. Supershrink.

HUGO *gives a clenched-fist sign and winks at* EDDIE. *He goes out.* EDDIE *and* BRENDA *are left there.* BRENDA *half-smiles at* EDDIE, *picks up some of the debris from the table, goes out to the kitchen.* EDDIE *throws himself into a chair.*

EDDIE. Oh bloody Mary.

Scene Four

MARY's *room.* MARY *kneels, head down, on the mattress. Knock at the door. Another knock. Then the door opens, and* LAURENCE *comes in.* MARY *kneels up. She looks at* LAURENCE. *She's frightened.*

LAURENCE. I have come. I have come to say I'm sorry.

Pause. MARY *frozen with fear.*

I've come to say I'm sorry 'bout the paintings.

Pause. MARY *looks at him.*

Come to make it up with you.

He goes to MARY, *and, rather clumsily, puts his arms round her and kisses her on the cheek.*

There.

MARY *suddenly pushes at him.*

MARY. You *can't* do that.

LAURENCE. What?

MARY. Not children any more!

LAURENCE. Uh, came to —

MARY (*quite viciously, crowing*). He says he wants to come to bed with me. He came into my room. We got to tell the doctor.

LAURENCE. Uh?

MARY. I mean, we're just not children *any more*.

LAURENCE. I only . . .

Upset, LAURENCE *stands and goes to the door, turns back*.

Came to say . . .

He turns and goes out, slams the door. MARY *lies back, rather self-confident*.

MARY. I mean. I mean to say.

Slight pause.

I had to lock the door, you were away. I had to lock the door.

Slight pause.

Quite a relief, they came, in their white coats, with jacket, for you, long white jacket, with long arms and bits of string. A great relief.

Pause.

And so you went inside.

Slight pause.

You've gone inside.

In great pain.

And you won't melt inside.

BLACKOUT.

Scene Five

LIGHTS *on main area*. BRENDA *enters with cups of coffee. Puts them down*. EDDIE *stands, goes and starts rolling up the canvases on the floor*.

BRENDA. D'you want some coffee?

Pause. BRENDA *goes and helps* EDDIE.

We can put some up again. When this dies down.

Pause.

Don't worry 'bout it.

EDDIE (*busy rolling*). Of course, what she is saying, through her pictures, something on the lines of, love me, love my paintings. Please. If it's no trouble.

BRENDA. Yuh.

EDDIE. She is saying things that she can't find the words for. Take them down, and you have struck her dumb.

BRENDA. Oh, sure.

EDDIE *looks at* BRENDA. *Then he picks up the rolled canvasses, piles them on a chair.*

Of course, what she is doing is invading people, through her pictures. Something on the lines of, taking over. So the argument would run.

EDDIE. She has been stigmatized.

BRENDA. Yuh, sure.

EDDIE. By all of you.

Pause. BRENDA *a slight laugh.*

What's funny?

BRENDA. This is funny. This place. Our, unsacred family.

EDDIE. Our what?

BRENDA. With its rules and hierarchies. Rituals and scapegoats and taboos. Its Holy Fathers and its Mothers of Invention. Brother hoods and sisters of wild mercy. Its involuntary incest and its unforbidden fruits. And acid will be taken on the terrace after dinner. And the child-like will be heard but never seen.

EDDIE. You what?

BRENDA. I just, just sometimes, wonder it it's possible at all. Do you?

EDDIE. Well, certainly, this nuthouse isn't big enough for . . .

BRENDA. No.

She turns to the stairs. MARY *stands there, naked, covered from head to foot in her own shit.*

Uh . . .

She turns back. EDDIE *hasn't noticed.*

Uh, Eddie . . .

EDDIE. What?

BRENDA. It's Mary.

EDDIE *turns. Sees* MARY.

EDDIE. Oh, yuh. So it is.

BRENDA. Um, she's . . .

EDDIE. Oh, yuh. She's covered in her shit. No, doubt about it.
Shit, is it. Could tell a mile off.

Pause. He looks at his watch.

Yup. That's the stuff she's covered in. Well, now, it's ten of
ten, I think I'll just go . . . Yuh.

He walks to the exit.

MARY. Eddie.

EDDIE *stops, doesn't turn.*

Eddie.

Pause.

You are my goodness, Eddie.

Pause.

EDDIE (*not turning*). Oh my Mary.

He walks out left. BRENDA *doesn't know what to do.* MARY
stands. Pause. EDDIE *comes back in with half an onion and a
pot of honey and a spoon. He thrusts the onion at* MARY.

EDDIE. OK, monster, put that in your mouth.

MARY *puts the onion in her mouth.*

OK, now, creature. Spit it out.

MARY *spits it out.* EDDIE *spoons a spoonful of honey.*

Now that is badness coming out. And this —

He puts the spoon in MARY's *mouth.*

Is goodness going in.

MARY *stands there, the spoon in her mouth.*

That's better? Good. Now, monster, creature from the black
lagoon . . .

MARY *a slight smile behind the spoon.*

We better clean you up.

Bang of doors. DOUGLAS *and* BETH *re-enter. They are slightly merry. They see* EDDIE *but not* MARY.

DOUGLAS. Well, that was all most pleasant. Hallo, Eddie, Brenda. How's the —

BRENDA *nods to* MARY. DOUGLAS *sees* MARY. EDDIE *goes to* MARY, *and takes her hand. They walk hand in hand to the stairs. They start to climb.* DOUGLAS *looks again to* BRENDA.

BRENDA. She that takes upon herself, the shit of the whole world.

She goes out. BLACKOUT.

Scene Six

Immediately, in the DARKNESS, *a mantra is sung.* LIGHTS. *Main area. Mantra goes on. Enter* DOUGLAS. *He carries a suit jacket, waistcoat, and tie on a hanger, a pair of black shoes and a suitcase. The mantra stops. He looks off right. Then he takes off his sweater and suede shoes. He is putting on his tie as* BRENDA *enters, with three fresh bottles of milk. He looks at* BRENDA. *He finishes his tie, puts on his waistcoat, jacket and shoes.* BRENDA *goes out. The mantra restarts.* DOUGLAS *looks off right.* DOUGLAS *puts the sweater, suedes and hanger in the suitcase, picks it up and goes out.* BLACKOUT *and the mantra goes on.*

Scene Seven

LIGHTS. *Main area. The mantra ends. Luggage in the room.* BETH *sits reading.* BRENDA *packing things in a case on the table.* EDDIE *comes in left, a slightly nervous grin at the two* WOMEN, *goes out to the stairs.*

BETH. Hey, did she eat today?

BRENDA. She drank some water.

BETH. Yuh. D'you think she —

BRENDA. Very thin.

BETH. Sure is. Hugo says, she has this kind of instinct, stops her going off the edge.

BRENDA. So we must hope.

BETH. Yuh. Sure.

Pause. BETH looks at her watch, stands.

Well, have lots of fun. I have to go into my trance right now.

Exit BETH right. BRENDA packing. Re-enter EDDIE from the stairs.

BRENDA. All right?

EDDIE. So-so. She kind of waved.

BRENDA. It's only for three weeks.

EDDIE. It's only for three weeks.

BRENDA. You want to share a cab?

EDDIE. Sure, thanks.

BRENDA. I'll ring for one.

She goes out left, taking her suitcase. EDDIE checks his passport and travel documents. Enter HUGO from the kitchen, in a pinny.

HUGO. You on your way?

EDDIE. Yuh —

HUGO. Everything in order?

EDDIE (*pockets passport*). Yuh. Look, Hugo —

HUGO. No.

Pause. He goes and shakes EDDIE's hand.

Send me a dirty postcard.

EDDIE grins, picks up his luggage.

It's bitter, acrid, tastes like piss, but she has got to drink it. From the inside, roll away the stone.

Slight pause. EDDIE shrugs.

EDDIE. Oh me of little faith.

BLACKOUT *and a* SPOT *hits* BETH.

BETH. I give you the end of a golden string
Only wind it into a ball
It will lead you in at Heaven's gate
Built in Jerusalem's wall

BLACKOUT *and a Gregorian Chant covers the change.*

Scene Eight.

MARY. *Main area. Paper on the floor. She kneels on the paper.*

MARY. Remember, as a child, strange feelings. Feel apart. Not here, not anywhere, a thing. All clumpy, weary. Head all big and fuzzy. Bits of me.

Pause. She picks up a crayon. Starts to draw. Then she suddenly starts talking, playing people in the drawing.

Hey. You.
Hey, get a move on.
Heavy.
Hey, you, come on. Move.
It's heavy, clumping up the hill. Like feet in treacle. Mustin't fall.
Come on. Don't whine. We haven't got all day.
Clump clump. Clump clump. We're there.
The top. The silver sky.

All right then, pass the hammer.
One. Two. THREE.

Dead thing. The dead don't feel.

Long pause. MARY still.

I'm blown apart. There's bits of me.
All floating to the other side. A leg, an arm. I'm on the moon.
Another.

Pause. She starts to draw again.

Hey, you.
Who, me?
You don't know what you're doing.
Listen, what he says. We don't know what we're doing!
Hur hur hur.
Hey, you.
Who me?
I'm telling you. Today, you're going to heaven. One of you.
Oh, yuh? Big deal. Which one? Hur hur.
Hey, you.
Who, me?
I'm thirsty.

Drink it up, then. Like a good boy.
Drink it up.

No, no. The sky's gone crimson.
God oh God why have you . . .

Long pause. MARY still.

And the urge to spew it out, the bomb. But more you tear at it, the more it seems to cling, to stick inside you. Got to lie with it, and work it through.

Pause. She starts to draw again.

Hey, you!
You up there. Come down.
If you're so great, so clever, come on down.
He can't.
Well, ask him why. Can whisper.
Can't. Can't talk.
He's sulking, in a paddy. Cos he can't come down.
I won't.
I won't come down.
Stay in the dark.

Pause.

Be empty. Nothing. Void. Hang on.

Pause. Then a SPOT fades up on HUGO.
Hold MARY's light.

HUGO. Petrifying.

Pause.

'Mean, so bloody thin.
Just on the edge.

Pause. HUGO goes to MARY. His spot fades.

Oh, Mary, must you suffer so.

Pause. MARY looks up, to HUGO. In some surprise, she realizes.

MARY. No. Wrong. Not suffering.
No more. It's you who's suffering.
Not me. It's you who's stretched and bleeding, up against the golden sky.

Pause. HUGO goes out.

Not finished. Not alone.
You're not the only one.
Not on my own.

BLACKOUT, *and at once, in the* DARKNESS, *a door slams, and* LIGHTS *snap up again. Enter* ANGIE, *who is 20, dressed in white jeans, a sweater, beads round her neck, carries a placard*

"US OUT". She is tired but strangely over-energized. She throws the placard down. She throws herself into a chair.

ANGIE. Hey. Hey. LBJ.

She pulls her shoes off, tosses them across the room, anywhere. She sticks her feet out, apart, twiddles her toes.

Ho. Ho. Ho. Chi Minh.

She looks at her feet. Then, suddenly a terrible pain on her face, something pent up in her energy has been released. She pisses herself. It runs down the legs of the chair. In hopeless disgust, she murmurs:

Oh. Oh, no.

*Her head goes down. She crumples to the floor. A moment. Then MARY BARNES crawls to ANGIE. She puts her arm round ANGIE.
LIGHTS fade to darkness.*

Act Three

Scene One

LIGHTS *on the main area.* MARY.

MARY. Story. I wrote. There was once a tree in the forest who
felt very sad and lonely for her trunk was hollow and her head
was lost in mist. Sometimes the mist seemed so thick that her
head felt divided from her trunk. To the other trees she appeared
quite strong, but rather aloof, for no wind ever sent her
branches to them. She felt that if she bent she would break,
yet she grew so tired of standing up straight. So it was with
relief that in a mighty storm she was thrown to the ground. The
tree was split, her branches scattered, her roots torn up and her
bark was charred and blackened. She felt stunned, and though
her head was clear of the mist, she felt her sap dry as she felt
her deadness revealed when the hollow of her trunk was open
to the sky. The other trees looked down and gasped, and
didn't quite know whether to turn their branches politely away,
or whether to try and cover her emptiness and blackness with
their green and brown. The tree moaned for her own life,
and feared to be suffocated by theirs. She felt she wanted to
lay bare and open to the wind and the rain and the sun, and
that in time she would grow up again, full and brown, from the
ground. So it was, that with the wetness of the rain she put down
new roots, and by the warmth of the sun she stretched forth
new wood. In the wind her branches bent to other trees, and
as their leaves rustled and whispered in the dark, and in the
light, the tree felt loved, and laughed with life.

Her branches, bent, to other trees.

BLACKOUT.

Scene Two

LIGHTS *on main area.* ANGIE.

ANGIE. Angie came to the house, in 1968. She'd known some
people, round the place. Then she'd freaked out in, of all places,
Iran, which can be rather dodgy. So someone flew out, to bring
her back. She was really smashed. Angie's father was a Brigadier-
General. Her brother was a stockbroker. Her mother was a
Justice of the Peace. Her lover was a Maoist. It did not make

for a stable and happy home environment. Bit of a cliché, really: straight family with radical chick. What wasn't a cliché was that background-versus-boyfriend was driving her right out of the little her breeding had left of her mind.

She sits.

If you say to someone, often, dear you don't mean that, eventually they're going to believe it. Become drained. If you say to someone, frequently, that what they do is not their nature, then their nature gets a mite confused. Remade. Becomes a second nature. Whose am I. If you say these things to someone, constantly, they end up living in response to other people, all the time.

She lights a cigarette.

When she was 14, her mother bought her a blouse. It was three sizes too big. It was extremely ugly. She couldn't change it. She wore it, and she felt ashamed. The blouse demonstrated how ugly she was. It showed that her bosom was too small. She didn't fit the blouse. When she was 16, told her father she believed in free abortion on demand. This shocked him rigid. Sanctity of life. He was a General. A fucking Army General. His *job*, desanctifying life.

When she was 21, Paul — the Maoist lover — told her that she'd never be a real Communist because of her conditioning. He told her that she'd never be a real revolutionary cos of something — which he called the Roedean Factor — which would stop her really hating those from whence she came. To really, hate, her mother. And he told her, that as soon as they returned from Persia, he was going to ditch her for some soft-Trot proletarian in Sunderland or Leeds and settle down.

Pause. She stubs out her cigarette.

If you take someone's thoughts and feelings away, bit by bit, consistently, then they have nothing left, except some gritty, gnawing, shitty little instinct, down there, somewhere, worming round the gut, but so far down, so hidden, it's impossible to find.

Longer pause.

Imagine, if you will, a worldwide conspiracy to deny the existence of the colour yellow. And whenever you saw yellow, they told you, no, that isn't yellow, what the fuck's yellow? Eventually, whenever you saw yellow, you would say: that isn't yellow, course it isn't, blue or green or purple, or . . . You'd say it, yes it is, it's yellow, and become increasingly hysterical, and then go quite berserk.

There's an awful lot of sand in Iran.

BLACKOUT.

Scene Three

MARY's *room.* MARY *sits on her bed.* ANGIE *sits on a chair, her head down. Beside her, on the floor, a pile of academic books, a pen, a ringfile. Silence a few moments.*

MARY. Hey, Angie. Angie.

ANGIE (*looks up*). Yuh?

MARY. I got a book. My stories. Want to read?

> ANGIE *nods.* MARY *gives her the made-up book.* ANGIE *looks at it a moment. Then she tosses it back on the bed. Head down. Pause.*

MARY. Hey, Angie, want to lie down?

ANGIE. No.

MARY. OK.

> *Pause. Then* ANGIE *looks up.*

ANGIE. Hey, Mary? Could you kill your mother?

MARY. I did, in my heart.

ANGIE. Yuh, no, I mean really. Blow her up. One afternoon. At tea. Bits of mother, floating in the milk-jug, dribbling down the wall.

> *Slight pause.*

It'd be like suicide.

MARY. I know.

ANGIE. Be like you killed yourself.

MARY. I've felt like that too.

> *Pause.*

ANGIE. I was born with a Caesarian. From my mother's womb untimely ripped. Hail Caesar. Ha!

> *Pause. She breathes deeply. Gets herself together.*

Now, Mary, got to read. I got to write this essay.

MARY. Angie, no.

ANGIE (*picking up a book*). The daily tasks, we must complete.

MARY. No, Angie —

ANGIE. Hey, don't you bug me, Mary, now, OK? I gotta read.

> *She picks up the ringfile and a pen to take notes. She opens the book and reads a bit. Then she lights a cigarette. Reads some more.*

> Hey. Cop a load of this. "I is another. I am present at the flowering of my own ideas. I watch them, listen to them, it is wrong to say I think, I ought to say, I Am Being Thought". The poet Rimbaud. Rather good.

> *Pause. She takes a drag. Then her head whips down and the book and the ring-file fall. Pause.*

> What did you do?

MARY. Went down.

ANGIE. Like how?

MARY. When I was frightened that I'd kill myself, I'd lie down, in the dark, for weeks, see no-one. Hold the anger in myself. Like as if cross-legged, or something. Hold yourself in pain.

ANGIE (*head up*). Oh. Kind of yoga.

MARY. All religions.

ANGIE. Opiate. Um.

> *Pause.*

> In Iran, I thought I was giving birth to baby Jesus. Quite impossible, of course, because I'm barren. Cunt is like a dust-bowl. Running sore.

> *Pause. She stubs the cigarette out in the wastepaper basket.*

> I am alienated from my means of reproduction. Ha!

> *Pause.*

> I wanna be in the dark. Put ashes on myself.

MARY. I know. I felt that too.

> *Pause.*

ANGIE. Look, Mary, I ought to go ring Max. Tell him, come over.

MARY. Oh, Angie, why?

ANGIE. We're working on this pamphlet. It consists, you will be staggered to gather, of a critique of the capitalist system.

MARY. Oh, Angie, no.

ANGIE. Also, I usually take a little sexual intercourse at this hour. Ha!

MARY (*whispers*). No.

ANGIE. A fucking sandpit.

Pause.

What's that? That noise?

MARY. It's just the dustbinmen.

ANGIE. They're emptying my cunt.

MARY. You feel that they're inside you.

ANGIE. Yuh.

MARY. I felt that too. I felt that everything was me. And nothing. Eddie, me. And Eddie went away, I went away. The only thing to do was lie down with my anger, keep quite still, and it dissolves.

ANGIE. It does?

MARY. Eventually.

ANGIE. I feel that everything, is going on inside my head. A thousand armies, are manoeuvering, around my brain.

Pause. She goes and sits on the mattress next to MARY.

A hundred thousand little yellow men. Manoeuvering.

Slight pause.

I wish they'd melt away.

Suddenly, she picks up the waste-paper basket and empties it over her head. Lots of nasties. Pause.

Should I have done that?

MARY. Yes, you should.

Pause. ANGIE rubs the stuff in her face. She picks a cigarette butt out of her hair. She eats it. Pause.

ANGIE. Eaten it.

MARY. I understand that.

ANGIE. Do you?

MARY. Course. I felt like that. I used to eat my shits.

ANGIE. Wow. What d'it taste like?

MARY. Just like shit.

Pause.

ANGIE. Mary, I gotta go ring Max.

MARY. No, mustn't go.

ANGIE. Look, Mary, not just Max. The fucking revolution.

MARY. No, that's not the real thing. You must go down.

ANGIE. Go down.

Long pause.

Hey, Mary.

MARY. Yes?

ANGIE. Gimme your rosary. I want to hold it.

MARY *gives* ANGIE *her rosary.* MARY *cradles* ANGIE. *Long pause.*

MARY. This is the important thing.

ANGIE *suddenly tightens. She pushes* MARY *away.*

Angie?

ANGIE. No. No. *No.*

ANGIE *up, to the washbasin, splashes water over her face.*

MARY. Angie . . .

ANGIE, *her face still dripping, finds a comb, and, combing her hair, runs out.* MARY *up.*

Oh . . . Oh, *no.*

LIGHTS *on downstage as* MARY *leaves her room after* ANGIE. ANGIE *then enters from the stairs, and runs across. She bumps into* EDDIE *who enters left eating a sandwich.*

EDDIE. Hey, Angie, how's it go?

ANGIE. I gotta PHONE.

She runs out left.

EDDIE. You gotta phone.

MARY *enters from stairs. To* EDDIE.

MARY. Eddie, quick —

EDDIE. Hey, hey, what goes on?

MARY (*trying to pull* EDDIE *towards the left*). It's Angie, she's trying to phone —

EDDIE. Why shouldn't she?

MARY (*still pulling*). Oh, cos she's got to go down Eddie —

EDDIE. Mary. Stop that.

Pause. MARY *lets* EDDIE *go.*

MARY. But —

EDDIE. Listen. P'raps you're right. But musn't force her, do what you did. What she wants. OK?

Slight pause.

Just let her, what she wants to. Different from you.

ANGIE *has reappeared from left.*

ANGIE. Now that is true. I'm definitely different.

Pause. She walks across to the stairs, mumbling.

Differ. Diff. Erent. Defer. Defence.

She goes out. MARY *looks at* EDDIE, *who makes a vague, non-committal gesture.* MARY *runs out after* ANGIE. EDDIE *goes out.* LIGHTS *downstairs fade, as* ANGIE *comes into* MARY's *room. Enter* MARY *behind her.* ANGIE *sits on the bed. She puts the rosary round her neck.*

ANGIE. So did you really feel like me?

MARY. I did.

MARY *sits on the bed.*

ANGIE. It's awful.

MARY. Yes, it is.

ANGIE. I rang my mother.

MARY. Did you?

ANGIE (*crying*) Cos I fucking love her, don't I? Motherfucking mother. Hurt my mother, she hurts me.

MARY. I don't.

ANGIE. You don't . . .

MARY. Don't hurt you.

ANGIE *looks at* MARY. *She's stopped crying.*

ANGIE. Oh, I like it here.

MARY. You do?

ANGIE. Yuh. Do.

Pause.

Gimme your tit.

MARY *gives* ANGIE *her breast, cradling her in her arms.*

You are my mother, Mary.

Long pause. ANGIE *down, lets* MARY's *breast go.* MARY *sits there, looking at* ANGIE.

MARY. I am your Mother Mary.

BLACKOUT *and White Rabbit by Jefferson Airplane covers the change.*

Scene Four

Fade White Rabbit, and, in the darkness, we hear PEOPLE *singing.*

Happy Birthday to you
Happy birthday to you
Happy birthday dear (Angie
                (Angela
Happy birthday to you.

LIGHTS. *The* PEOPLE *are applauding. They are* HUGO, BRENDA, *upstage, and downstage* ANGIE's MOTHER *and* BROTHER, *standing either side of* ANGIE, *who sits in front of a small table with a birthday cake on it. She is eating a piece of cake. The* OTHERS *have pieces of cake or cups of tea.*

MOTHER. Your father was so sorry he couldn't be here.

ANGIE. Oh. Yuh.

MOTHER. But he sends you lots of love.

ANGIE. Oh, thank him, please.

MOTHER. Of course.

Slight pause. The MOTHER *gestures at the* BROTHER, *who queries, realizes and goes out. Pause.*

Lovely cake.

ANGIE. It's smashing. Brenda made it.

MOTHER. I must get the recipe.

Pause.

This is your main living area, is it?

BRENDA. Yes, that's right. We eat, and things, in here.

MOTHER. It's good and spacey.

BRENDA. Yup.

Re-enter the BROTHER *with a parcelled present.*

MOTHER. Ah. Here we are.

ANGIE. Oh. Me?

MOTHER (*smiles*). Who else?

ANGIE *smiles. She takes the parcel, opens it. It's a print dress. It is obviously highly fashionable, expensive and much to* ANGIE's *taste.*

ANGIE. Oh, it's lovely.

MOTHER. Do you like it?

ANGIE. Oh, that's really nice. Hey, can I try it on?

MOTHER. Of course you can.

ANGIE *gets up, shows the dress to* HUGO *and* BRENDA.

Hey, look at this.

BRENDA. It's very pretty.

ANGIE. Oh, I must . . . Hold on a minute.

She's going to the stairs exit.

MOTHER. Darling, I'll come with you.

ANGIE. Fine.

MOTHER. So, while we're at it, we can get you packed.

Pause.

Your things.

HUGO. Um —

ANGIE. Don't want to go.

MOTHER. Darling, that's not true.

ANGIE. Don't want to be with you.

MOTHER. Now, Angela, you don't mean that.

ANGIE. I do, I hate it, being with you.

MOTHER. Look, darling, I don't mind it when you say that, cos I know that you can't help it.

ANGIE. I can help it.

MOTHER. If I thought that you weren't ill, I'd be so angry.

Pause.

We only came because you asked us to.

Pause. ANGIE *shrugs. Exit* ANGIE *and her* MOTHER. *The* BROTHER *doesn't look at* HUGO *or* BRENDA.

HUGO. Where were you thinking of taking her?

BROTHER. She rang my mother up.

HUGO. That doesn't quite answer the question.

Pause.

BROTHER. I imagine she strikes you as something of a paradigm, my mum. Bit of a classic, really. She will wear those hats. She will get so up-tight when people cut her off from her own daughter, will get so upset when people say that Angie's illness is her fault. That she has driven her own daughter to distraction.

BRENDA. Well, that isn't —

BROTHER. Isn't it? You tell her that.

Pause.

It's obvious that Angela's in pain. She's suffering. The treatment stops the suffering.

HUGO. Now, look —

ANGIE *and her* MOTHER *come in.* ANGIE *wears an expensive overcoat that doesn't go with her sweater and jeans. Her* MOTHER *carries her suitcase.*

BROTHER. So where's the dress?

MOTHER. She decided not to wear it, for the drive.

BROTHER. Oh, yes.

HUGO. Um —

MOTHER *turns to* HUGO.

I'd like to ask you to leave Angie with us, for a while.

Slight pause.

I would really like you to consider that possibility.

MOTHER. You'll upset her.

HUGO. *We'll* upset her?

MOTHER. Angela is ill. Needs curing.

HUGO. Look, curing, with respect, is what one does to bacon.

MOTHER. Bacon?

HUGO. Not to human beings.

Pause.

MOTHER. She's been eating cigarettes.

Pause.

Now, shall we, please —

ANGIE. Where's Mary?

MOTHER. Mary?

BRENDA. Mary's out.

MOTHER. Who's Mary?

ANGIE. Mary . . . lives here, in the house.

Pause. The BROTHER *picks up the luggage.*

BROTHER. I'll go and load the car.

He goes to the door, but decides to wait as ANGIE, *after a pause, goes to* BRENDA, *kisses her. She goes to* HUGO, *kisses him. Then she notices she's still wearing the rosary. She takes it off and gives it to* HUGO.

ANGIE. There's rosary. That's for remembrance.

She laughs. Then stops. Then, with an odd little clenched fist sign, she walks out.

Ho. Ho. Ho.

She goes, followed by her BROTHER. *The* MOTHER *smiles at* HUGO *and* BRENDA, *as if* ANGIE's *odd behaviour confirmed her view. She makes to go.*

BRENDA (*suddenly, a step forward*). First break two dozen eggs —

MOTHER *turns back, interrupts, quite genuine.*

MOTHER. No, please. It's hard enough. Please don't.

She goes out. Pause.

BRENDA. Come the great day, she will be the first.

Suddenly, HUGO *runs out right.*

Hugo?

No reply. A moment, then re-enter HUGO. *He's pulling on a pair of suit trousers, he carries a jacket, a tie, and a pair of black shoes. He sits and puts the shoes on.*

BRENDA. What you doing?

HUGO. Going after.

BRENDA. Where?

HUGO (*stands, pulling on his jacket*). The hospital. Only one of three.

BRENDA. To get her back?

HUGO's *running to the door, tying his tie.*

HUGO. To try and get her back.

He's gone. BLACKOUT, and the end of White Rabbit covers the change.

Scene Five

LIGHTS *on main area. EDDIE stands looking at the debris of the tea party. He can't work it out. Door slam and enter MARY.*

EDDIE. Well, hallo, horror.

MARY. Hey, guess who?

EDDIE. I can't.

Enter ZIMMERMAN.

Hey, Zimmerman —

MARY. And guess *what* —

EDDIE. I can't. Hey, Zimmer-

MARY. GUESS.

EDDIE. You've been elected Pope.

MARY. No, no!

EDDIE. I've been elected Pope.

MARY. Oh, Eddie.

To ZIMMERMAN.

You tell him.

ZIMMERMAN. Who, me?

MARY (*going out up the stairs*). Yes, you!

EDDIE. Well?

ZIMMERMAN. Glad tidings of great joy. Having made one of herself for so long, Miss Barnes has now got herself an exhibition.

EDDIE. What?

ZIMMERMAN (*Takes a letter from his pocket*). A one-loon show. Peruse.

He gives the letter to EDDIE, *who reads it.*

EDDIE. That's wonderful.

Enter MARY, *carrying a large number of canvases and bits of paper. She drops them on the table.*

MARY. Right now. This is some of them.

ZIMMERMAN. Hey, Mary —

MARY. Mean, for a start.

ZIMMERMAN. Um, a gallery. Small gallery. Not Wembley Stadium.

MARY. The triptych! Eddie, come on, give a hand.

ZIMMERMAN *has picked up a painting on a plank of wood.*

ZIMMERMAN. Now, how do I frame that?

MARY *has noticed* HUGO, *who has entered left. She's about to go and tell him her news, but his face stops her.* HUGO *takes off his tie.* EDDIE *and* ZIMMERMAN *still looking at the paintings.*

EDDIE. Hey, this one has to go.

ZIMMERMAN. Which is that?

HUGO *goes to* MARY *and gives her the rosary. The* OTHERS *notice, and look at* MARY *and* HUGO.

HUGO. Our family, was not quite strong enough. Compete against the family that's in her head, her family.

He goes out.

MARY. Eddie.

EDDIE (*not clear what's going on*). Yuh?

MARY. I want to —

EDDIE. Yuh?

MARY. Please, Eddie, find my brother. Want to go down with my brother.

BLACKOUT. *A modern jazz record fades up to cover the change.*

Scene Six

*The music goes on. Screens have been set in front of the main area.
On the screens are hung or projected three of MARY's paintings.
Spots on either side of the stage, in front of the screens. On one
side MARY, dressed for the occasion, holding a glass of wine. On
the other side, also holding a glass of wine, a neat, middle-aged
man in an uncomfortable suit.*

MARY. Hallo, Simon.

> *The MAN turns. It is the PATIENT of the first scene, MARY's
> brother SIMON.*

SIMON. Good evening, Mary.

MARY. Thanks for coming, Simon.

SIMON. Not at all.

MARY. It's really smashing, isn't it?

SIMON. I am so pleased for you.

> *Pause. EDDIE enters behind MARY with a glass of wine.*

MARY. Oh, Simon, will you come and stay with us? At least, to
come and see us?

> *Pause.*

SIMON. I used to paint. Before my illness. I haven't done so much,
since then.

> *Pause.*

I'll come one afternoon and visit you. But not to stay.

> *He smiles at MARY and goes out. MARY bites her lip, turns to
> EDDIE.*

EDDIE. Don't smother him, OK?

> *They go out as BLACKOUT.
> Judy Driscoll's Colours covers the change.*

Scene Seven

*MARY's room. Tea is laid out, with a pot, cups and cakes. EDDIE
sits on a cushion on the floor. MARY sits on her mattress. SIMON
sits on the only chair. The MEN drink tea, MARY drinks milk.
Pause.*

MARY. Would you like a cake?

SIMON. No thank you. I have a meal back at the hostel.

MARY. How is the hostel?

SIMON. It is very pleasant. I have my own room.

MARY. Not in the chronic ward, no more.

SIMON. No, not in the chronic ward. But still, they give me my depixol.

Pause. SIMON *sips his tea.*

EDDIE. Are you working, Mr Barnes?

SIMON. Yes, I'm working in a factory.

EDDIE. What doing?

SIMON. Oh, I cut up bits of metal to make coils.

MARY. Kind of electrical.

SIMON. That's right.

Pause. SIMON *sips his tea.*

It's better than my last job.

Slight pause.

EDDIE. What was —

MARY. Simon — Eddie, Hugo, everybody here, they could look after you.

Slight pause.

They did for me. They saved me. They could do the same.

Slight pause.

Simon, we're from the same womb. We got all twisted up together. But things can get untwisted. Really.

Slight pause. More desperately.

Simon, was a girl, here, in the house, was getting better, really better, and they came and took her to the hospital and smashed her up like . . .

She breaks.

Simon, come and stay here. PLEASE. Why won't you understand what's best for you?

Pause.

SIMON. Is there a lavatory?

MARY. Yes, across the corridor. I'll show you.

SIMON *puts down his cup*, MARY *gets up, takes* SIMON *out.
A moment.* EDDIE *puts his cup down, stands.* MARY *enters,
in some passion, and bashes* EDDIE *on the chest.*

EDDIE. Hey, what's that for?

MARY. Eddie, Simon's cutting up bits of metal. It's not making
him better, he's still on drugs, why don't you make him come
here?

EDDIE. Make him?

MARY. He looks like wax, a robot. Disappearing. Make him stop.
Make him go down.

EDDIE. Can't make him.

MARY. Why not?

EDDIE. Cos he may not want to.

Pause.

You do what you want to.

MARY. Oh, I do so want him to be better.

EDDIE. You're greedy for him to be better. You want to eat him
being better.

MARY. Oh, Eddie, why d'I feel so bad.

EDDIE. Because you're angry with me and you want to kill me
because I won't make Simon be like you.

MARY. Not angry with you, Eddie.

EDDIE. Aren't you?

Pause.

MARY. I want him to become himself.

EDDIE. Who's that?

MARY *turns away. Pause.*

Hey, Mary.

MARY. Mm?

EDDIE. You know, I said you're greedy. But you're not the
greediest.

MARY. Mm? What?

EDDIE. There's someone who's much greedier than you.

MARY. Yuh? Who?

EDDIE. That's me. That's Eddie. I'm the one that's greedier than you.

Pause. MARY smiles.
Then SIMON comes in. EDDIE stands.

EDDIE. Right, I think I ought to go.

SIMON. I must go soon, too. Ten minutes.

EDDIE. Good to see you. Hope you come again.

EDDIE and SIMON shake hands. Exit EDDIE. SIMON sits.

MARY. I'm glad you like the hostel.

SIMON. Mm.

MARY. I'm sorry, shouted.

SIMON. Mm.

MARY. I hope you'll come and visit me again.

SIMON. I shall.

Pause.

MARY. I've changed. You see that?

SIMON. Yes, you've changed.

Pause.

I've no foundation.

MARY. But you, but you could . . .

She stops herself. Pause.

SIMON. In fact. In fact. I've given in my notice.

MARY. Oh, Simon, have you?

SIMON. Yes. In fact, I'm thinking about changing my accommo-
dation. Can't eat meat. I want a place where I can make my own
food.

MARY. Oh, Simon, you can do that . . .

Slight pause.

Cook my own food here.

SIMON. You do?

MARY nods slowly.

I will think about it, moving here. If I fit in.

He stands, notices there's paint on his coat.

I've something on my coat.

MARY *jumps up.*

MARY. Oh that's it's paint, it must have come off . . . Look, I'll find some turps . . .

SIMON. It's on my coat.

MARY *rushes round, finds turps and a cloth, dabs* SIMON's *coat.*

MARY. It's coming off.

As she works, a little laugh.

My room's an awful mess. I don't know how it gets this way, however much I . . . There, it's gone.

MARY *stands.*

SIMON. I think it's gone.

MARY. Your own room wouldn't be like that, of course. That would be tidy, as you like.

SIMON *stands there. Pause.*

SIMON. They. Give me. Have these tremors from the depixol injections. So they give me disipal, to counteract. And to make me sleep, the mogadon.

Pause.

Mary, when I came into your room, that night, before I went away, I wans't going to have sex with you. I just wanted to touch you, that's all.

He picks up his scarf, puts on coat.

I'll have to get a certificate. I'll need it, for the people, if I'm coming here.

He goes out. BLACKOUT.

Scene Eight

A single source LIGHT. *Main area, on the record-player. It's night.* LAURENCE *sits in front of the record player, he's playing a record: Helter Skelter by the Beatles. He turns it up louder. He shakes about. He turns it up louder.* SIMON *appears, in a dressing-gown and slippers over pyjamas buttoned up to the neck. He watches* LAURENCE. LAURENCE *turns the music louder.* SIMON *puts his hand to his head.* LAURENCE *turns the music even louder.* SIMON *turns, walks out.* LAURENCE *turns the music even louder.* BLACKOUT. *Music on a few moments, very loud, then an awful scratching noise as the record is ripped off, followed by smashing metal and wood, followed by the broken record-player being thrown on the floor.*

Scene Nine

LIGHTS. LAURENCE *stands downstage. The broken bits of the record player are at his feet.* BRENDA *and* MARY *stand.* HUGO, EDDIE *and* ZIMMERMAN *sitting.*

LAURENCE. I'm sorry.

BRENDA. Not your fault.

LAURENCE. I made him go away. Too noisy.

HUGO. Not your fault.

> LAURENCE *kicks the record-player bits.*

LAURENCE. I like the noise. He couldn't stand it. Sorry.

> *Exit* LAURENCE *right. Pause.*

MARY. He just, wanted to be left alone. Be quiet, to make his food, and eat it, do the things he does, precisely, organize his day. He wasn't taking tablets any more. He wasn't taking drugs.

HUGO. He'll come back.

MARY. Gone. This is the END.

HUGO. It's not the end.

MARY. He'll be destroyed.

BRENDA. Mary, Simon's different, he hasn't got your painting and your writing —

MARY. Painting? Writing? That's not important. What's important is my brother. And you helping.

> *She shouts at the* OTHERS.

You know him better than he knows himself!

EDDIE. You know that isn't true.

MARY. It's just the same as Angie. You just let them go.

HUGO. Oh, shut up, Mary.

MARY. The lot of you. You're therapists, aren't you? You're healers, aren't you? Well, then, do your job. And CURE HIM.

EDDIE. Oh, for Christ's sake, Mary . . .

MARY. Oh, I'm so angry with you, Eddie —

EDDIE. Are you? Are you angry?

MARY. Yes!

EDDIE. Then say it —

MARY. I am angry —

EDDIE. Once again —

MARY. I am very angry with you, Eddie —

EDDIE. Knock, who's there —

MARY. It's MARY —

EDDIE. Mary who —

MARY. IT'S MARY BARNES!

   Pause.

EDDIE. That's good.

MARY. Oh, I'm so *angry* with you, Eddie!

   MARY *storms out. The* OTHERS *smile.*

EDDIE. Very good indeed . . .

   Pause.

ZIMMERMAN. Will her brother come back?

EDDIE. May do. It's not for long.

ZIMMERMAN. Why not?

BRENDA. We're moving out. The lease expires.

ZIMMERMAN. Can't you extend?

HUGO. The worthy burghers wouldn't wear it.

ZIMMERMAN. What'll happen?

EDDIE. Simon will stay in mental hospital. Why not? It's his
   career. His job. His place in life.

   Pause.

ZIMMERMAN. Mary once told me a long and rather rambling tale
   about her masturbating. One could say without fear of
   contradiction that her clitoral attitude was ambivalent. This
   seemed partly due to the fact that, before she came here, she
   was going to the shrink on Monday, told her it was fine, you

carry on, and then on Tuesday, to confession, where they told her she was in a state of mortal sin.

EDDIE. And so?

ZIMMERMAN. I just wondered, what you thought, on opening her soul, to find the Catholic cross still etched across her heart. That's all.

Pause.

EDDIE. That's how she is. That is her journey. That is real and right and true for her. That's all.

Slight pause.

She's better than she was. And she is better without shocks or drugs or anything. That's all.

Slight pause.

It's possible. That's all.

Slight pause.

It's not my job, my place, to tell her how to run her life. Or anyone.

Exit EDDIE. *Pause.*

ZIMMERMAN. I liked it when the students went to Washington, and hummed a mantra, tried to levitate the Pentagon. Good image. Liked it when we dropped a little acid, and convinced ourselves the secret sacred gardens in our heads were somehow blooming all across the cosmos. A nice, analogy.

HUGO *stands.*

HUGO (*with a little smile*). I think I liked it, very much, when Lyndon Johnson went on television, and announced he'd not seek re-election. Liked it very much when all the wretched of the earth, the great unwashed, made LBJ give up his second seal for peace. I liked that, metaphor. I think, I think it was the very best. You know.

He goes out.

ZIMMERMAN. When do you leave?

BRENDA. First week in May.

ZIMMERMAN. What do you think will happen?

BRENDA. I don't know.

ZIMMERMAN *says nothing.*

I know . . . I think I know . . .

Pause.

For me, it was best of all . . . Just see ourselves, each other, all our, lumpy nakedness. To hear our voices, all their, I don't know, their rasping melody.

Capture our lives in all their, well, their messy majesty.

You see?

ZIMMERMAN. Of course I see.

BRENDA. We didn't build the future. But we are no longer, other, to ourselves.

Pause. With a smile.

We've closed the door behind us. And, who knows, what lies beyond, the point, beyond the pale.

She goes out, up the stairs. ZIMMERMAN *stays there. He sees* SIMON, *standing with his suitcase, having entered from the street.*

ZIMMERMAN. Ah. Hallo.

BLACKOUT. *During the change, No More Heroes, by the Stranglers. Dust sheets are thrown over the furniture in the room.*

Scene Ten

Then, in the darkness, a crash, of glass and breaking wood. A shaft of LIGHT on the empty stage. It is some years later. Enter KEITH and ANGIE. They have just broken in. ANGIE, who is dressed rather formally, brushes herself down. KEITH is in contemporary clothes.

KEITH. Well, this is it.

Pause.

We used to play, our group, we used to play through there, along the corridor.

ANGIE *looks round.*

Mean anything?

ANGIE *shakes her head.*

ANGIE. Don't think so.

KEITH. Don't think so.

Slight pause.

Look, you did live here?

ANGIE. Yes, I'm sure. I had this pocket book, you see, with lots of names, addresses, and afterwards I couldn't quite remember them, and so I went round, looking, trying to reconstruct it, bit by bit.

KEITH. You found the people?

ANGIE. No. They'd moved on, all of them.

KEITH. Except this place.

ANGIE. That's right.

Pause.

KEITH. They must have wiped you out.

ANGIE. They did.

Pause.

The shocks. You see, it's like a photograph. Before, it's there, and then you look again, it's faded. Just a blur. It's odd, you feel much better.

KEITH. Better?

ANGIE. Lets you forget, the things that hurt you, I suppose. It takes you back. Back to the comfort that you knew before.

Slight pause.

Better get back. My mother will expect me.

Pause. KEITH *shrugs, as if to apologise for* ANGIE's *not remembering the place.*

Thank you so much for showing me. It's tricky on the A to Z. The streets don't quite look, how they are.

KEITH. Well, things have changed round here. They're changing all the time. Most of the places that were here, not any more.

ANGIE. Except this place?

KEITH. That's right.

ANGIE *smiles. She makes to go.*

You know, the people round here, us, so frightened of the people in this place. They threatened us. Disrupted our, uncomfortable security.

ANGIE. I'm sorry?